UNEXPECTED

what to do
when life
disrupts
your plans

Stephen & Karen Blandino

To Our Family, Friends & Church

Thank you for walking with us
when life disrupted our plans.
We love you!

Praise for
Unexpected: What to Do When Life Disrupts Your Plans

"An invaluable, honest and practical look at how we should respond when unexpected disruptions happen in our lives. This affirming message of hope and healing is a must read!"

John McKinzie, Lead Pastor, Hope Fellowship, Frisco, Texas

"When life disrupts your plans—and it will—how will you respond? Karen and Stephen Blandino have walked through deep valleys of disruption and emerged with truth that will help you face your own times of pain and loss. Take advantage of their hard-won perspective for facing the unexpected setbacks and traumas in your own life."

Dr. Daniel Allen, Leadership Coach and author of
Summoned: Stepping Up to Live and Lead with Jesus

"Stephen and Karen say we actively avoid disruptions. I do! And yet this book clearly shows that we need not do this. Instead, we need to embrace these interruptions as God showing up just for us. The Blandinos clearly show that God uses life's disruptions to bring true meaning and purpose into our lives. I was blessed by this book, and you will be too."

Dr. Kathleen Patterson, Professor and Director of the
Doctorate of Strategic Leadership Program for the
School of Business and Leadership at Regent University

"No matter what side of life's disruption you're on, you will treasure this book. It is authentic, practical, eye-opening, effective, and encouraging. You don't have a choice when it comes to life's unexpected disruptions, but this may just be what you need to get through it."

Dan Hunter, Lead Pastor, Living Church, Mansfield, Texas

"The 'grace stories' of others uplift and encourage us. Stephen and Karen Blandino have written a wonderful book that does just that. You'll find yourself inspired, encouraged, and feeling hope as you live out the 'grace walk' we call the Christian life. Life lessons abound in *Unexpected: What to Do When Life Disrupts Your Plans.*

Dr. LeRoy Bartel, Dean for the College of Bible and Church Ministries, Southwestern Assemblies of God University, Waxahachie, Texas

"Everyone, and I mean everyone, faces unexpected events at some point in their life. You're probably either coming out of a crisis, in one, or getting ready to experience one. Wherever you find yourself, the principles Stephen and Karen share through their own stories will give you the tools to navigate those unexpected moments that catch you by surprise."

John Davidson, Spiritual Formation Pastor, The Oaks Fellowship, Red Oak, Texas

"I want to recommend *Unexpected: What to Do When Life Disrupts Your Plans.* Stephen & Karen Blandino provide fantastic encouragement, coaching, and practical steps to deal with circumstances in life that disrupt our plans. The '7 takeaways' alone, are worth the price of the book. And if you're a pastor, church planter, or ministry leader, this book would be a great foundation for a sermon series or small group study."

Dave McNaughton, Church Planting Catalyst and Coach, and Team Leader for Church Multiplication Network

TABLE OF CONTENTS

INTRODUCTION

If someone were to ask you, "What plans do you have for your life?" you'd probably start talking about some objective or goal, a dream that makes your eyes light up just thinking about it. Your voice might start going up and down, as you talk faster and use your hands, describing the job you want, the relationships you desire, the success you imagine.

What you probably *wouldn't* talk about would be all the disruptions you're expecting along the way. All those roadblocks life throws into your path that seem to delay, derail — perhaps even dismantle — all those wonderful plans of yours.

Most of us actively try to avoid disruptions. When someone interrupts your concentration at work, it can be irritating, especially if they're keeping you from moving an important project forward. When you're headed to work and you come up on a traffic jam, if you're anything like me, you immediately start looking for a neighborhood side street you might explore for an alternate route. But there's a difference between disruptions to our schedules… and disruptions to our lives.

Life is imprinted with all manner of bright spots and pleasant memories: celebrations, achievements, milestones. But it's also scarred by hurts and pain, detours we never saw coming and certainly wouldn't have asked for. Some are big and some are small, but none of them are "expected." Sometimes it feels like it's raining rocks, and we're doing our best to dodge a fatal blow.

In fact, so certain is this basic truth that Jesus warned us about it in John 16:33: "In this world, you will have trouble." There are almost as many different possibilities as there are people: losing a job, receiving a bad report from a doctor, a tragic accident, a late-night phone call. Pain shows up in all kinds of forms: a relationship ending, a financial setback, even (God forbid) the death of a loved one. And what do most of these events have in common? They're unexpected. They're disruptions to the things we've hoped for, dreamed we might become. Life isn't always good.

But when life unexpectedly disrupts our plans, it's up to us to decide how we'll choose to respond. You may have spent literally years of stacking one good decision after another, carefully placing each one just so, like the bricks that will make up your life. Even when you're careful, even when you have a plan, disruptions can still materialize out of nowhere, simply showing up uninvited on your doorstep. We may not have control over disruptions, but we can absolutely control what we do when — not *if* — they happen.

Disruptions can also occur more organically, those natural consequences that often simply result from our own poor choices. (You spend money like there's no tomorrow, and then your house goes into foreclosure because you can't make the payments.) But no matter whether your setback was entirely avoidable or completely inevitable, either way, disruptions still hurt.

How we respond to a disruption reveals a great deal about us. More importantly, that response can pave the road to where we'll end up next. Good responses tend to bring healing, hope, and opportunity. Bad responses usually spiral us into still more disruptions. We may not have control over disruptions, but we can control *what we do* when they show up.

In the pages that follow, Karen and I will be telling you our personal stories about the unexpected. We'll also be sharing seven life principles that these experiences have taught us. While we want you to find hope in our stories, more than that, we want to equip you with ideas that can help you navigate your way through your own disruptions to a place of peace.

Hurt is real. Pain is a legitimate side effect of going through adversity. And although it may be difficult to see it this way when you're in the middle of a trial, how you respond to your pain is even more important than the reality of that pain. We hope to show you how you can consistently respond in a positive way to the inevitable disruptions life throws at us all.

And that's an important point: we're all on this same journey together. What Karen and I sincerely desire for you is that you discover greater freedom, deeper healing, and eventually, wholeness. The only way out… is *through*. But we're here with you. So let's get started!

SECTION 1
Unexpected Disruptions

CHAPTER 1
Karen's Unexpected Disruption: Stolen Peace

It was October 17th, 1989. Many people remember that night because of the infamous earthquake that struck before game three of the World Series between the Oakland Athletics and the San Francisco Giants. Even as Oakland was sweeping the series, the Loma Prieta Earthquake forced a ten-day delay between games three and four. While everyone else was watching that unexpected earthquake happen live on television, my own unexpected crisis was about to shift the earth beneath my feet.

It was a cool, windy evening in Texas. Stephen and I were dating at the time, and we had spent the evening studying together in the library at a local community college. We had both graduated from high school in 1987, and we were working our way through our basic courses in college. My parents weren't home that night because they were enjoying a few days of well-deserved vacation in Tennessee, so Stephen followed me home in his car to make sure I got there safely. When I got to my house, I parked in the garage, told Stephen good night, and pushed the button to close the garage door as I went inside. As soon as the garage door was all the way down, Stephen left for his house in a nearby neighborhood, about five minutes away.

I walked straight to my room, put away my books, and turned on the TV. I was planning to spend the night at my cousin's house, so I packed my overnight bag while a sitcom played in the background. When I finished packing, I went to take a quick shower before heading over to my cousin's.

I was alone in the house, and I had left the bathroom door slightly ajar, when suddenly I heard loud noises, like a kind of banging. I was still in the shower, and I thought maybe my brother had come home. His name is Roy, but our family nickname for him was Bobo. I called out:

"Bobo? Is that you?"

I stood there under the falling water for a moment, listening, but no one answered back. I pulled the top edge of the shower curtain back slightly and peeked out around the side. There, through the cracked door, I could see a pair of eyes peering back at me from the darkened hallway. I did not recognize that face. I instinctively tried to reach out to close the door, but before I could even process what was happening, two men flung the door wide open and barged in. One man jerked the shower curtain back while the other man put a gun to my head. They dragged me out of the bathroom, naked and flailing and kicking and screaming and scratching.

When they got me out the door, I could see down the hallway into the living room. Three other young men were in the process of dismantling our stereo and television system, in between shuffling in and out the front door with jewelry boxes in their arms. My mind reeled as I tried to process the chaotic scene.

Then the man with the gun pointed it at my face and demanded, "Where's the good stuff?!?"

I must not have been thinking very clearly, because instead of trying to answer, I shot back, "Where's my brother?!? What have you done with my brother?!?"

Then in fear and desperation, I cried out, "In the name of Jesus, take anything you want, but leave me alone! In the name of Jesus, take anything you want, but leave me alone!"

One man jerked the shower curtain back while the other man put a gun to my head. They dragged me out of the bathroom, naked and flailing and kicking and screaming and scratching.

An image flashed in my mind of the shoebox full of one-dollar bills that my mom had in her closet. I darted to her closet, grabbed a robe and pulled it on, took out the box of money, and gave it to one of the men.

He jerked it from my hands and peeked under the lid. Thinking it was more money than it really was, he glanced at the other guy and nodded, and they both ran out.

As soon as they left, I ran over to the phone and called 9-1-1. But when the operator answered, my heart sank as she began by apologizing: "I'm sorry, ma'am, we don't serve your area. You'll need to contact your local police."

Of course I had no idea what the number was for our local police, and I couldn't think straight, so instead of looking for it, I frantically dialed the first number that popped into my head: my cousin, who, fortunately, lived just a few minutes away.

As soon as he picked up, I blurted out, "I was just robbed at the house. Five guys just robbed me."

"I'll be right there!" He darted to his car and was at our house within minutes. He ran in and found me, made sure I was okay, then looked up the number for the police.

To this very day, I sometimes have this recurring dream that I'm trying to call somebody… but I can't reach them.

Home Sweet... Crime Scene?

It was only a few minutes between the time my cousin called the police and when they arrived. They started sorting out the situation immediately, asking questions and investigating the scene. Our front door was hanging open, splintered, and our living room was a dismantled mess. As I talked with the police and my mind began to slow down, gradually we began piecing everything together. While I was in the shower, five young men kicked in the front door. Most likely, they were trying to disassemble our entertainment center when I cried out, tipping them off that they weren't alone. And of course it was right after that that the two guys came and pulled me out of the shower.

While I was still talking with the police, my cousin called Stephen. When his phone rang, Stephen figured I was probably calling to see if he had heard about the earthquake in San Francisco. But when he picked up, he heard my cousin's voice instead. "You need to get over here quick. Karen's been robbed."

Stephen was there almost immediately. My cousin brought him to me in my brother's room, where I was sitting on Bobo's bed. Stephen came straight to me, and I grabbed the front of his shirt and pulled him close, sobbing into his chest. "Please don't ever leave me. Please don't ever leave me. Please don't ever leave me," I pleaded. He cradled me, doing his best to comfort me in this crisis.

After he had given me some time to get my cry out and to regain my composure, Stephen called our pastor. The police were still collecting fingerprints, drifting in now and again to ask me more questions, when our pastor arrived. He comforted me and prayed with us both.

When the police were finished, I headed to my cousin's house to spend the night with his family. We were finally able to reach my parents in Tennessee, and they immediately loaded up their car to race home.

I hardly slept that night at my cousin's house. Every time I tried to close my eyes, images flashed in my mind of the five young men who had stolen my peace. As the adrenaline subsided, it took with it all of the comfort I had felt first at seeing my cousin, then the police, then Stephen, and then our pastor. And in its place, devastation came pouring in to fill that void.

The police eventually caught up with all five of the young men who had robbed our house. All of them were teenagers. As each one was

> **Every time I tried to close my eyes, images flashed in my mind of the five young men who had stolen my peace.**

picked up, the full story of that night came together. They had decided together to commit a house robbery. They stole a car from another neighborhood, then drove around for awhile before finally targeting our house. They pulled up to our house in the stolen car, stopped out front... and kicked in the door. The oldest boy, the one who held the gun on me, was sentenced to prison, where he is still, even as I am writing this. Each of the younger ones ended up serving at least some time in juvenile detention. Years later, one of the boys was convicted of killing a man, a crime for which he was sentenced to death.

He Restores My Soul

When I reflect back now on all that happened that night, what I see in hindsight is God's amazing hand of protection on my life. Yes, it was bad — horrible, really. But you know, things could have been worse. So. Much. Worse. My arm was bruised where the boy had grabbed me to drag me out of the shower. But other than that one, temporary mark, physically, I was completely okay.

In subsequent years, when I'd have to meet with investigators to discuss my case, they were always shocked to learn that I wasn't raped or beaten. They used words like "lucky." Of course I know better. My life was spared. And so much more. While it was terrifying as it was happening, and I suffered through emotional pain afterwards — losing my sense of safety, keeping my mind from exploring the infinite "What if…?" scenarios, and so on — I still consider it a miracle, and even a gift, really, that I have my life.

When life disrupts your plans with unexpected events, you need encouragement. You need support. You need other people who can help

> While it was terrifying as it was happening, and I suffered through emotional pain afterwards – losing my sense of safety, keeping my mind from exploring the infinite "What if…?" scenarios, and so on – I still consider it a miracle, and even a gift, really, that I have my life.

you get through it. You need to be able to find a path that will lead you to your healing. We'll talk more about all of those things in just a little bit. But first, I want you to experience Stephen's story.

CHAPTER 2
Stephen's Unexpected Disruption: A Broken Heart

Sunday, March 16, 2014, was a chilly morning for Texas, as I was getting ready to head out to 7 City Church. Karen and I had planted this new church eighteen months earlier, in the booming West 7th cultural arts area of Fort Worth. God was doing amazing things, blessings we hadn't even thought to ask Him for, and we were thrilled to get to experience hearts and relationships thriving in our new church community. Just nine months in, we hired a full-time associate pastor, Klen Kuruvilla. And with an incredible team of volunteers backing us, in September 2013, we even launched a second service. Most importantly, God was changing lives.

Of course I had no way of knowing it then, but that Sunday in

March would turn out to be a defining moment in my life. Karen had been fighting a severe sinus infection for two weeks, so she had stayed home to rest that morning. I was just glad that she was finally on the mend and grateful to see her strength gradually returning.

I wrapped up a teaching series that morning at 7 City called "Winning the War Within." Little did I know that my own battle was just about to begin. After our morning services, we were going to host a lunch for our guests at a nearby restaurant. I walked outside to get in my car when all of a sudden the cold air felt like it was burning my lungs. It was really strange, and certainly not normal, but nothing I would have called "alarming." I brushed it off, headed to the restaurant, and enjoyed meeting several new people who had recently started attending 7 City. It was a great day!

I can't say exactly when it began, but I was on a collision course with congestive heart failure.

After lunch, I walked briskly back to my car in the parking garage near the restaurant. Once again, I could feel the cold air burning my lungs. I didn't realize it yet, but the opening salvo had been fired in a war within my body. My lungs were in the process of filling slowly with liquid, and when that cold air hit that fluid, it created a burning sensation. I can't say exactly when it began, but I was on a collision course with congestive heart failure.

Fifteen years earlier, I had been diagnosed with mitral valve prolapse (MVP) while we were living in Lexington, Kentucky. "MVP" is a condition affecting roughly three percent of the population. I'll spare you all of the medical jargon, but put simply, "MVP" means your heart's mitral valve doesn't close properly.

I was fortunate. In my case, my family doctor spotted unusual heart rhythms during a normal office visit. He said I was probably born with the heart defect, and he recommended I see a cardiologist for an annual check-up. When we moved back to Texas, I found a cardiologist who conducted a battery of tests. Eventually he referred me to yet another doctor, who conducted more tests and prescribed a medication that I take every day. When he retired, I met Dr. Parrish, my current cardiologist. Dr. Parrish conducted an EKG and Echocardiogram for good measure. I began seeing him once a year, with the caveat that if I ever noticed anything unusual — shortness of breath, irregular heart rate, and a few other, lesser indicators — I should let him know as soon as possible.

Year after year, (thankfully!) the results to my Echocardiogram always came back the same: no change. That was a good thing. Dr. Parrish believed that I would need surgery eventually, but "not until changes in my condition were noticeable." My last heart checkup was just nine days before the events of March 16th. And, once again, everything came back the same as always: "all is well."

But on that Sunday afternoon in mid-March, changes in my condition would suddenly become noticeable — very noticeable. Unexpected snuck up behind me and put me in a headlock. Even though we had a great morning at 7 City, and an equally great lunch, I could feel my energy starting to fade. I went home, figuring I just needed to get some rest. As the afternoon progressed on into evening, I started wondering if I might be coming down with something more serious, like the flu. I drank some coffee and took a hot shower, and that helped a little bit. But I was also starting to cough.

I remember asking Dr. Parrish once how I would know if I needed surgery. He said that the most likely indicator would be that I'd notice an immediate shortness of breath. While my breathing was certainly becoming more difficult, it didn't feel like anything too serious. While I was coughing more and more, I wasn't having any trouble catching my breath.

Karen wondered aloud if maybe we should go to the ER, just so I could get checked out. (Doesn't it seem like sickness *always* strikes on weekends, when all the normal doctors' offices are closed?) We checked my pulse rate, but it seemed to be within the range of normal. And besides, since Karen was only just then getting over her own two-week illness, I wanted both of us to get plenty of rest.

When I woke up around 6:00 am on Monday, things were worse — *much* worse. I sat up in bed and told Karen, "I think you need to take me to the ER." A relatively smaller branch of a hospital ER had recently opened just a few miles from our house. We had been there just a couple of weeks earlier, when Karen's sinus infection was at its worst, so we knew they could get us in quickly. We threw on some clothes and jumped in the car.

Within just a few minutes of our arrival, the ER doctor had me on oxygen. They also took blood cultures, administered an EKG, and started me on an IV with antibiotics. After a short while, the doctor looked me over and asked, "Are you *sure* this just started yesterday afternoon?"

"Yes," I assured him. I told him again about feeling that cold blast of air deep inside my chest Sunday afternoon, and about how I felt progressively worse throughout the evening.

He scrunched up his face, and I could hear genuine concern in his voice. "Something serious is going on. I think you might have pneumonia." His assessment was based on the condition of my lungs. "You're very sick. We're not going to be able to treat you here," he said. "We need to get you to Harris Southwest or Harris Downtown right away. We'll call an ambulance to transport you. Which hospital do you prefer?"

My first instinct was Harris Downtown. It's a larger hospital, so I reasoned they probably had more available resources. But without hesitating, Karen answered, "Harris Southwest."

As it turned out, that was God's providence.

A Series of Unfortunate Events

Although I was still feeling terrible, they at least had me stabilized by the time the ambulance arrived in the early afternoon. We went straight to Harris Hospital Southwest, where a medical team was already waiting for us. As they wheeled me in, they were peppering both me and Karen with questions. After a short while, once again, a doctor asked, "Are you *sure* this just started *yesterday afternoon?*"

"Yes," I told them. My associate pastor, Klen, had arrived just a few minutes earlier. "Ask him," I said, motioning to Klen. "He was with me all morning, and through lunch."

By now, breathing was getting really difficult. Everyone in the room could see that I was visibly straining, gasping for each breath. The best way I could describe it is I felt like I was drowning. They suspected pneumonia. Of course I was hooked up to all kinds of equipment, so one of them asked me about my irregular heartbeat.

"I have mitral valve prolapse," I explained. "But I had my annual checkup just last week, and everything was good."

Then I added, almost as an afterthought, "My cardiologist is Dr. Parrish. His office is in this hospital."

The team ordered an Echocardiogram, and someone immediately went off to call Dr. Parrish. By 3:30 that afternoon, Dr. Parrish showed up to listen to my heart. I could tell he was concerned, but if he thought my situation was legitimately dangerous, he wasn't letting on yet. He said simply, "I'm going to order an Echocardiogram."

"Oh, they already did one," I told him.

Within minutes, someone had brought him my results. He looked them over carefully, and then, with urgency in his voice, Dr. Parrish told me, "You don't have pneumonia. One of the cords to your mitral valve has snapped. This is serious. You need heart surgery. I'm calling CareFlite to have you transported immediately to the Heart Center downtown."

> **Dr. Parrish: "You don't have pneumonia. One of the cords to your mitral valve has snapped. This is serious. You need heart surgery. I'm calling CareFlite to have you transported immediately to the Heart Center downtown."**

(CareFlite® is a specialized medical transport service in Texas, essentially an air ambulance.)

"When will my surgery be?" I asked, trying to take it all in.

"That's the problem," he said. "Your lungs have filled with fluid, which means you're not in any condition to have surgery. We've got to get that fluid off your lungs first. Perhaps your surgery will be on Thursday."

Upon this news, the pace of everything around me immediately surged into fast forward. The whole team taking care of me sprang into action. A nurse warned me I might need to be intubated.

"Are you okay with that?" he asked.

I didn't even have to think about it. "Well, it's better than dying," I said.

It seemed like just minutes later that the CareFlite team came streaming into my room, each of them zipping through their designated tasks with maximum efficiency. It was clear they knew exactly what they were doing, that they had done it before... and that *they were really good.* Their whole system is designed to prep you for transport and get you in the air as fast as possible. It hardly seems possible, but even in that flurry of activity, all of them somehow managed to keep reassuring me with amazing compassion.

One of them told me we were almost ready to go, which meant it was time for them to put me under. I reached out to Karen and our daughter Ashley, who were standing nearby.

"Stephen is simultaneously experiencing congestive heart failure and pulmonary failure. He's between a rock and a hard place."

I told them I loved them just before the CareFlite team sedated me and intubated me. Karen held my hand as they wheeled me out of the room. They loaded me on the helicopter and headed to the Heart Center at Harris Hospital downtown. Karen and Ashley immediately left to drive to Harris to meet me. Of course we got there long before they did. (Under different circumstances, I think I might have really enjoyed that helicopter ride.)

The next forty-eight hours were critical. While the surgical heart procedure I needed is pretty common, my particular set of circumstances was complicating everything. In fact, Dr. Parrish would tell us later that since 1996, he had only seen three or four mitral valves rupture. In most cases, they perform surgery long before MVP can get to this point. One of the worst factors, of course, was the compromised condition of my lungs.

At eight o'clock Monday night, Karen was in the waiting room when three doctors came out to talk to her. They told her, "Stephen is simultaneously experiencing congestive heart failure and pulmonary failure. He's between a rock and a hard place."

I needed heart surgery, but they couldn't start while I still had fluid on my lungs. That scenario could really only be a last resort. And as if things weren't dangerous enough, I also had a fever. They assured Karen that they would do their best to protect me from infection by getting that fluid drained as quickly as possible. If the night went well, they hoped to have me ready for surgery sometime the next day. If you'll remember, back at Harris Southwest, Dr. Parrish told me, "Thursday," but since then, they had realized my situation was even more urgent.

Karen told me later, "The most difficult night of my life was going home without you."

Monday night was a long, unsettling night for her. How could everything change so quickly? Sunday morning, she saw me leave the house looking and feeling completely healthy. But by the end of the very next day, I was fighting for my life. It was just too much, too fast. And I had promised her, all those years ago, "I'm not going to leave you."

Her emotional energy completely spent by the events of the day, Karen felt like her world was crumbling around her.

(A Little) Joy Comes in the Morning

When Karen arrived back at the hospital early Tuesday morning, my nurses greeted her with a little good news. They had successfully managed to drain two liters of fluid from my lungs during the night. While I still had a low-grade fever, there were no signs of infection, so the surgeons were willing to attempt heart surgery. They were all in agreement that was my best option.

At nine o'clock Tuesday morning, my pastors, Darius and Cindy Johnston, came to the hospital to see me. I was still sedated, all pale and unshaven and intubated. They stood on either side of my bed and prayed fervently for my healing. Karen would tell me later that it was one of the most emotional and powerful prayers she experienced in her entire life. It's good to have friends who will fight for you when you can't fight for yourself.

The doctors told Karen that my surgery would probably take between four and eight hours, but that if everything went extremely well, it could even take as little as two. There were just a lot of factors and a lot of moving parts to deal with. They needed to make repairs to my heart and strengthen my remaining cords. Depending on how you choose to look at it — fortunately or *un*fortunately — only fifteen percent of my mitral valve was salvageable, which meant they also needed to install a mechanical valve.

Karen, family, and friends sat anxiously in the surgery waiting area after my surgery began. They looked regularly at the tracking monitor for updates to my case. Every time my case number — ID #250373 — appeared on the monitor, it showed no change. Then, less than two hours after my surgery began, a nurse came out to the main waiting room and summoned our family and friends to a second waiting room for an update. Since I had only been in for a short time, and since they had somehow failed to update my case number on the waiting room monitor, most everyone was expecting bad news. The room hung heavy with fear and anticipation. Karen said those few extra minutes of waiting felt like hours.

Finally, Dr. Lin came in. His presence was reassuring. Not only had my surgery been a complete success, but my lungs were looking better too. He said they hoped they'd be able to get me off the ventilator on Wednesday — the next day — and that they'd probably be moving me out of ICU after just two or three days. There was a collective gasp, followed by smiles, emphatic thank-you's to Dr. Lin, and a spirit of worshipful gratitude to God. My pastor tweeted the news: "Thanks for prayers for @StephenBlandino. Dr. just reported surgery went great. Put in mechanical valve. Next few hours big for recovery."

Tuesday evening, Karen and Ashley got to come in to see me. Tubes, wires, and IV's were connected to my head, neck, chest, and arms. And I was a bionic man, with the official St. Jude Medical Device Identification Card (complete with serial and model number) to prove it. Wednesday evening, they took me off the ventilator. My only memory from Wednesday night was asking for my dad, and getting my intubation tube removed. (That's a fun experience if you're looking for something to do with your spare time on the weekends.)

My best memories from the whole event came on Thursday morning. When Dr. Parrish had first projected back at Harris Southwest that my surgery would happen on Thursday, I assumed I'd wake up in the hospital on Monday after my CareFlite ride. Instead, imagine how surprised (and delighted!) I was to wake up on Thursday — two and a half days later — with everything already done. Best of all, Karen came strolling in, grinning at me. I've never been so glad to see her.

I was out of the woods, but I still had a long way to go. In the coming days, I recovered slowly. The pain lessened, except when I coughed. Coughing felt like knives piercing my chest. My breathing continued improving as they kept removing fluid from my lungs.

A Parade of Miracles

As I look back on my heart failure, I can't help but feel awe at the cascade of miracles. It wasn't just one — that they got me into surgery and I survived — but it was several, an entire series, just one after another, each one feeding into the next. First, if we had gone to the ER too quickly, that first Sunday afternoon, it's possible they might simply have diagnosed me with the flu and sent us home. Karen told them to take me to Harris Southwest instead of Harris Downtown. That gave us immediate access to my cardiologist, a specialist who was able to diagnose what was actually happening.

Other things happened, too, that I haven't shared with

When you walk through a crisis, don't let the magnitude of your pain hide the miracle(s) in your pain.

you yet. I'll explain more later, but even how my family got to Fort Worth, and my parents' "just-in-time" arrival, were both amazing. The fact that pneumonia didn't set in (or any infection, for that matter) is a miracle. The doctors were able to drain two liters of fluid from my lungs just during that first night. That's a whole party's worth of Diet Coke! That cleared the way for them to perform my surgery Tuesday afternoon. Then the surgery went off without a hitch, completed even faster than their best-case scenario estimate. All of these are testaments to God's grace and power.

Finally, of course, there's the big one: I survived. I'm convinced that hundreds of people praying for me was what made the difference. After all that my family went through in the course of those four days, I simply cannot emphasize this enough: when you walk through a crisis, don't let the magnitude of your pain hide the miracle(s) in your pain.

On Monday, March 24th, 2014, I celebrated my 45th birthday. The next day, I was released from the hospital. I will never forget that birthday. And I'll never forget the unexpected event I faced just days before. God is faithful.

God taught Karen and me so much through these unexpected disruptions, my heart failure and her robbery. Now we're going to share with you seven takeaways we believe can help you better navigate those interruptions that happen in all of our lives. We'll tell you some more details from both of our stories and how they've played out since, which we hope you'll be able to use not just to overcome your pain, but to find hope again.

SECTION 2
What to Do When Life Disrupts Your Plans

CHAPTER 3
Prayer:
Tick-Tick-Tick and Fight, Fight, Fight

There's this old saying: "In a foxhole, there's no such thing as an atheist." Chances are good that even if you don't pray on a regular basis, when a crisis hits, that's when you start. And in those times, it's been my observation that the prayers most people lean on seem to fall into one of three categories. I call the first type "the bargain":

"Lord, if you'll get me out of this mess, I promise I'll never _____ again, and from now on, I'll always _____, forever and ever. Amen!"

The second type of prayer I've seen is a legitimate, genuine, desperate cry that God will intervene in your situation in some supernatural way. This type of prayer usually results when pain has driven you to the breaking point, that place of absolute surrender, of utter dependence on

God, where you literally have nowhere else to turn. This second type of prayer I call "the reliever":

"God, whatever it is you're trying to do here, I need your __peace__ / __relief__ / __comfort__ / _____. I'm just all out of ideas. I'm tired of resisting. I can't do anything else. Please... just show up."

While certainly there are many moments of beauty in this world, just as often, it can be a truly harsh environment. There's simply no denying that bad things happen to good people. When it feels like there's no justice, like the wrong people are getting blessed and the wrong people are getting hurt, when we just can't make sense of what God's up to, people often turn to the type of prayer I call "the question":

> **For most of us, when bad things happen, the pain we feel either drives us to God or away from him. But either way, the choice truly is ours.**

"God, why did you let this happen? Couldn't you have stopped it? Why didn't you? Don't you care what happens to us?"

Of course, the truth is, none of us are truly "good," at least not when we're held up to the light of God's standard. His holiness reveals my sinfulness, shining a light on how good God is... and on how bad I am. God is the ultimate model of goodness. No matter how good I may *think* I am, my goodness can't measure up to his.

For most of us, when bad things happen, the pain we feel either drives us *to* God or *away* from him. But either way, the choice truly is ours. And if we choose to run to God, usually the way we pray reveals how we're experiencing our pain. What kind of pray-er are you? Are you a bargain-maker? A pain-alleviator? A question-asker? The way you pray can tell you a lot about yourself. But there's another option...

"Thank You, Jesus"

Even looking back, it's hard for me to explain how I responded to God during my heart failure and immediately after. I wasn't trying to make bargains with God. I didn't intercede for my health, either. I wasn't crying out to him, passionately asking him to give me a miracle. (Honestly, I didn't have the strength to do those things.) I also never asked God, "Why?" I did pray, but for whatever reason, here's all that would come out:

"Thank you, Jesus."

Now, I'm no better than anybody else. Certainly I'm no spiritual giant. In fact, I'll bet there are people out there who believe that if my faith had just been a little stronger, none of this would have ever happened in the first place. But you know what? It did. And while my pain drove me to God, I wasn't in a place where I could ask him for anything. In some strange way, my unexpected pain was like a runway for the plane of gratitude to take flight. Those three words, "Thank you, Jesus," never left my soul. They defined me.

God didn't — and doesn't — owe me anything. The death and resurrection of His Son is more than enough. And in that moment, it just didn't seem right for me to try to make demands of Him.

When there was uncertainty: "Thank you, Jesus."

When I was struggling to breathe: "Thank you, Jesus."

When I experienced fleeting moments of relief: "Thank you, Jesus."

When we could tell I was finally on the road to recovery: "Thank you, Jesus."

When I came home from the hospital, my recovery included long daily walks — you know, all the way around our kitchen and living room. One of my favorite songs to listen to during those walks was "Great Are

You, Lord" by All Sons and Daughters. I don't know how many times I had already heard it when, one day, I was suddenly overcome with emotion as its simple, beautiful words pierced my soul:

You give life, You are love
You bring light to the darkness
You give hope, You restore
Every heart that is broken
Great are You, Lord

It's Your breath in our lungs
So we pour out our praise
We pour out our praise
It's Your breath in our lungs
So we pour out our praise to You only

It would be hard to explain why I connected so much with this song. There's so much going on it. I think part of it is that I know what it feels like to struggle for your next breath. Then the next one. And then the one after that. I know what it's like to have that thought: *What if this is it? Could this be my end?* There was nothing *I* could do. If something was going to happen, it was going to have to come from him. He gave me life. He brought light to my family. He gave us hope. He restored my heart that was broken — both literally and figuratively. He put breath, *his* breath, in my lungs. So my praise belongs only to him.

I stopped taking each breath for granted. As I walked by the refrigerator, tears began filling my eyes. I took another breath. As I walked around the corner of our kitchen table, my lip began to quiver. I took another breath. I finally leaned against the kitchen wall. I took another breath. And I sobbed. Have you ever thought about that? Realized just how extraordinary it is? That your body works that way? And that there's *breathable* air just *there?* Just readily available? It's miraculous, how he made us, all that he's given to us.

My lungs inflated with air, my heart pumped blood, and gratitude filled my soul. All I wanted to do was to spend, to give, to pour out whatever life I have left to honoring him. Worship became the language of my lungs. And all I could say was:

"Thank you, Jesus."

> **Worship became the language of my lungs. And all I could say was: "Thank you, Jesus."**

Tick-Tick-Tick

Some people might have gotten cabin fever convalescing at home. You know what I mean: when you feel like you can't be productive, and all you want is just to get out. I suppose I could have easily slipped into that mode, too. But the truth is, I wouldn't trade that time I got to spend with Karen, not for anything. My recovery gave us so much opportunity to talk. Even when she had to return to work, every single day we had some of the greatest conversations of our marriage (so far). Every one of those talks drew us together, bonding our hearts closer and closer to each other.

One night we were talking about my mechanical valve. When the house is really quiet, you can actually *hear* my valve working: *Tick-tick-tick-tick*. It sounds like a stopwatch embedded in my chest. Or as my rehab nurse once said to me, in that thick Scottish accent of hers, "You know what, Stephen? Apart from your ticker, you're fit as a fiddle!"

As Karen and I talked, I could feel myself being overcome with emotion once again. "Every *tick* is a reminder of God's faithfulness," I told her. It's like a surgically implanted gratitude gauge, constantly reminding me how good God is. But you know what it takes to hear it? *We have to get reeeeally quiet.*

When you're facing a crisis, when the world around you is falling apart, what's your *Tick-tick-tick?* What's that one thing you can cling to that reminds you of God's faithfulness? When uncertainty comes crashing in, when questions start racing into your mind one after another, can you get quiet? Can you find your *Tick-tick-tick,* that promise that quietly whispers to you, "Peace, be still"? When fear grips your heart, when unexpected disruptions impair your judgment, where do you go for that *Tick-tick-tick* that reminds you, "God is with me"? You need to find what that is in your life. He's promised you something. You need to find it, and you need to cling to it to help you weather the inevitable challenges that life's going to throw at you.

> **The God who walks with you before and after the storm is the same God who gives you the *Tick-tick-tick* during the storm.**

Tick-tick-tick drives you to prayer. *Tick-tick-tick* draws worship out of your soul. *Tick-tick-tick* reminds you you're not on this journey alone. God is with you. He has not forgotten you or abandoned you. The God who walks with you before and after the storm is the same God who gives you the *Tick-tick-tick* during the storm. His voice is quiet. But it's not silent. Are you listening? He's constantly reminding you that He is present, active, and faithful.

Tick-tick-tick…

Fight

A friend of mine once told me, "Stephen, as your ministry grows, you will reach a place where your prayers are simply not enough. You'll need a team of people to pray with you and for you." When we planted 7 City Church, that truth became more evident to me, but nothing drove it home more than heart failure.

When a crisis hits, it knocks the wind out of your sails. When "unexpected" shows up on your doorstep, you feel stripped of every ounce of strength. You feel violated. In those moments, you can't fight alone. You need others to stand with you, even for you, to fight — not physically, but spiritually in prayer.

I've often heard people say during a time of crisis that they "feel others' prayers." I now know what they mean. My prayers weren't enough. While I was praying, "Thank you, Jesus," someone else was stepping in to fight the battle. While praise was my prayer posture, fighting was the posture of countless friends and family members. And I positively *felt* it.

Some people stood by my side and prayed. Some sent text messages to Karen during the darkest hours, assuring her of their prayers. Ashley told me that people were praying from fourteen different countries around the world. My brother later told me that even friends in India were interceding on my behalf.

I don't know when, or how often, people prayed. I'm sure some were one-time prayers. Others did what the Apostle Paul said: "Pray continually" (1 Thessalonians 5:17). No matter how great or small, long or short, every prayer was heard by God, and every prayer made a difference. I'm simply thankful that others were willing to fight when I couldn't.

When life disrupts your plans, who is standing in your corner? When a crisis hits your friend or your family, do you leave them to fight alone? A courteous, "I'll be praying for you," isn't enough. In the same way you need them, they need you. Sometimes we fight for one another, and sometimes we fight together for someone else.

Before and After the Storm Hits

The fight often begins *before* the storm hits. The Sunday morning before the robbery, I [Karen] asked my pastor to pray for me during a church service. What was strange to me was the length of time my pastor spent praying for me. I had no idea what my week would hold, but I believe God was preparing (and protecting) me for the events that were yet to unfold. His prayer was like a spiritual and physical shelter *before* the storm hit.

On March 4th, exactly two weeks before Stephen's surgery, he received a text message from a friend he hadn't heard from in years:

"Hey Stephen, the Lord has been dropping you on my heart lately. Praying for you, bro!"

Eight days later, he texted him again:

"How are you doing today? Anything I can be praying about?"

God used this friend to fight for Stephen in prayer before his heart ever failed. Like seeds sown in fertile soil, these prayers were sown before the storm clouds even gathered. *Before the storm* prayers are proactive prayers.

Even when the critical hours of Stephen's surgery had passed, people still prayed. Nearly three weeks after his surgery, he was struggling with fatigue. His progress seemed slow, and at times it felt like his recovery was on pause. I sent a text message to nearly thirty friends and family with specific things to pray about. That day was the best day of Stephen's recovery up until that point. He didn't take a nap until the end of the day, and he felt his strength returning at a faster rate.

Being "specific" in prayer is actually one of the lessons I've learned in this journey. I often sent text messages to people with updates on Stephen's condition, along with specific prayer requests. Several people later told me, "Thank you for being so specific in your updates and prayer requests. It helped me know exactly how to pray for Stephen." Crises aren't a time for generalizations. Specific needs require specific prayers.

Several weeks after being home, Karen showed me [Stephen] all of the comments shared on social media during the time of my surgery. I had no idea how many people had prayed for me. That night I posted these words:

"Tonight Karen shared with me hundreds of Facebook comments from people who prayed for me before, during, and after my heart surgery. I am simply overwhelmed. Words are not enough to say thank you to so many of you who prayed for me, Karen, and Ashley, especially in the most critical hours. God heard your prayers. God answered. He is good and faithful."

Thinking of (vs. Praying for) You

One day Stephen received a card from a lady who has faced her own fair share of battles… not just for weeks or months, but literally for years. Her faith is strong as she fights relentlessly for her loved one.

What caught our attention about this particular card was the word she had scratched out. The card said, "I believe that the thoughts of those who care about you can make a difference." But she had scratched out the word "thoughts" and written in the word "prayers" in its place. The inside of the card read, "That's why I want you to know I'm thinking of you and hoping that each new day will be a little easier for you." Again, she had scratched out "thinking of" and replaced it with "praying for."

When I saw the card, I said, "I get that." When Stephen was in the hospital, I didn't just want people to think about him; I wanted people to pray for him. Prayer was what was going to make the difference — not "happy thoughts." No matter how well-meaning they might be, simple thoughts don't have the power to positively influence someone else's circumstances. But prayer does.

When you're facing a crisis, you need people who will surround you with loving support and encouragement. We'll talk more about that later. But you need more than their thoughts; you need their prayers. And when you're fighting for a friend, co-worker, neighbor, or loved one, they need you to do more than just "think about them." They need you to fight. Prayer is your fighting posture.

Takeaway #1

So what's the first takeaway when life disrupts your plans? It's simply this: **Use prayer as worship and as a weapon when the unexpected appears.** Prayer calibrates your heart toward gratitude. In the middle of despair, we can say, "Thank you, Jesus." Prayer adjusts our hearts to that *Tick-tick-tick* of God's faithfulness.

> **"Do not be anxious about anything, but in every situation, by prayer and petition, with thanksgiving, present your requests to God." (Philippians 4:6)**

Prayer is also a weapon. It's what we use to fight for others, and it's what others use to fight for us. Ephesians 6:12 says, "For we are not fighting against flesh-and-blood enemies, but against evil rulers and authorities of the unseen world, against mighty powers in this dark world, and against evil spirits in the heavenly places" (NLT).

So if "unexpected" has made an "unwanted" appearance in your life, pray. Let your heart be filled with worship to God. Seek others who will wield the spiritual weapon of prayer to fight with you and for you. And remember the words that Paul wrote to the church in Philippi: "Do not be anxious about anything, but in every situation, by prayer and petition, with thanksgiving, present your requests to God" (Philippians 4:6).

A Prayer for the Journey

Heavenly Father,
Thank you for not abandoning me in the middle of my pain.
Thank you for being an Anchor when the storm clouds are the darkest.
Today I choose to run to you, not away from you. I will walk through my
circumstances with a heart of gratitude. I will remember your
faithfulness, despite what my circumstances tell me. And I
will fight, and invite others to fight with me, through the
power of prayer. May you be honored in my life.
In Jesus' name I pray, amen.

CHAPTER 4
Trust:
Replace the Question with a Period

Trust in God is a phrase we throw around like free cotton candy at a carnival. It's a thing we say when we don't know what else to say. But when you're the one called to trust, it's a different story. Then it's not so easy.

Fear is the dominant emotion that dismantles our ability to trust God. Like a monster lurking in the closet of our minds, fear makes its presence known when the unexpected shows up.

When I [Karen] was robbed in my own home, everything I understood about peace was replaced with overwhelming fear. Loud noises still startle me and send my heart racing. Suspicious people put me on edge. Safety and security became my greatest comfort.

When Stephen's condition went from flu-like symptoms to fighting for his life in a matter of twelve hours, that same fear crept its way back into my mind. I remember driving home from the hospital Monday night with Ashley. I was dazed by the events of the day. How I made it home I still don't know.

When we got there, I fell asleep from sheer exhaustion. At midnight I woke up and emotionally fell apart. I called my mom and asked her, "Is he going to be all right?" She did her best to comfort me and reassure me that things would be fine. After I hung up the phone, I called my friend Jennifer and asked her the same question. I was sobbing so hard I could barely speak. Jennifer and her husband Derek held their breath as they wondered the worst. Finally I asked her the same question: "Is he going to be all right?" Jennifer assured me he would.

Fear is the dominant emotion that dismantles our ability to trust God. Like a monster lurking in the closet of our minds, fear makes its presence known when the unexpected shows up.

As soon as Jennifer hung up, she turned to Derek and told him, "I've got to go over there." She rushed to our house and stayed with me through the night. We talked and cried together. Finally she said, "Picture what it's going to be like. This is the worst day, but every day after this is going to be better. And one day, you know, Stephen's going to write a book about this." Jennifer is a true friend. She stayed the entire night, sleeping on a chair in our living room while I slept on the couch.

Replace the Question with a Period

During those first couple of days, God prompted me to change my perspective. Rather than asking, "Is he going to be all right?" God prompted me to drop that question mark and replace it with a period: "He's going to be all right... period." A simple shift in punctuation was the fragile beginning of a shift from fear to faith.

Less than two hours after Stephen went into surgery, somebody came to get us. "Mrs. Blandino, the doctor wants to meet with you," he said. Then he asked everyone to follow him to another waiting room. He gave no explanation and had little expression on his face. Everyone feared the worst as we waited for the doctor to arrive. That was the longest thirty minutes of my life.

I remember turning to a friend and saying, "If it was bad news, they would have asked me to step into a small, private room, right?" Again, fear was looming. I told Stephen's mom, "I just

> **A simple shift in punctuation was the fragile beginning of a shift from fear to faith.**

want him home. I just want him in my bed again. I just can't live without him." Fear was mocking me like a nightmare. Finally, at 3:42 pm, exactly two hours after the surgery began, the surgeon emerged with the news: "The surgery went great. The next twenty-four hours are critical."

An overwhelming sense of relief flooded that entire waiting room. Dozens of people waited patiently for the news, and finally a glimmer of hope peeked its head over the horizon.

That doesn't mean I never struggled with fear again. It was (and at times still is) a daily battle. I remember telling Stephen after he had been home for a couple of weeks, "I feel like I'm walking a tightrope, constantly hoping neither of us falls off." Fear is a terrible thing. It grips you with a vengeance as it sets up shop in the recesses of your mind, constantly generating questions to haunt you. But fear was never meant to define us, or our relationship with God. "For God has not given us a spirit of fear and timidity, but of power, love, and self-discipline" (2 Tim. 1:7, NLT). Trust is the journey God calls all of us to walk.

Facing My "Trust God Gap"

If you're like Karen and me, you probably bump into a certain "gap" in your life from time to time… perhaps more often than you'd like to admit. It's that gap between what I *expect* God to do and what He's *actually* doing. This gap is common when life disrupts your plans. I call this my "Trust God Gap." My Trust God Gap shows up when I ask myself, *"What does it mean to trust God in _____?"* where that blank is whatever I happen to be struggling to trust God with at that particular moment.

The "Trust God Gap" looks different for each of us. If you're trying to figure out what your Trust God Gap is, just answer this question: What does it mean to trust God in _____? Whatever you put in the blank is the label (or name) on your Trust God Gap. You might answer like this:

- What does it mean to trust God with my relationships?
- What does it mean to trust God with my job?
- What does it mean to trust God when someone mistreats me?
- What does it mean to trust God when somebody lies to me?
- What does it mean to trust God with my health?
- What does it mean to trust God with my money?
- What does it mean to trust God with my time?
- What does it mean to trust God with a really big decision?

I don't know what you put in your blank, but the good news is that God provides direction for your question, no matter what it is. Proverbs

3:5–7 says, "Trust in the Lord with all your heart and lean not on your own understanding; in all your ways acknowledge him, and he will make your paths straight. Do not be wise in your own eyes; fear the Lord and shun evil." There's a lot going on in these three simple verses. Let's unpack it together.

Trust in the Lord with all your heart — The word "trust" implies the idea of submissive helplessness. It's actually a picture of a servant who is waiting for his master's command so that he can respond in full obedience. In other words, the focus of trust is submission. The writer's advice is to submit your heart in full obedience to God.

Lean not on your own understanding — To *lean* is to prop yourself up against something. Our earthly wisdom (or understanding) cannot support the weight of our lives, challenges, pain, or disruptions. God's wisdom, on the other hand, is like a firm tree with deep roots, able to support the weight of our lives as we lean against him in full trust. Our wisdom is like a thin piece of balsa wood, simply too flimsy to prop up our lives. It's really easy to lean on your education, your success, your experience, your know-how. But those are the very things that often lead us out of God's will, especially if we've allowed them to get out of alignment with his Word.

In all your ways acknowledge him — To "acknowledge him" doesn't mean to give God his Sunday morning hour, or to say grace before all our meals. God wants us to invite Him into *every* area of our lives. Do you know what he means by "all"? That's not a trick question. All means all. Acknowledgement is an act of recognizing God's full Lordship in our lives.

He will make your paths straight — Our temptation (and our tendency) is to pick a path with the expectation that God will just rub-

God already has a chosen "bless-able" path for us. When we choose to trust him, lean on him, and acknowledge him, his path becomes clear.

ber-stamp approve it for us, like he'll shake his magic blessing dust over it or something. But that's not how God works. God already has a chosen "bless-able" path for us. When we choose to trust him, lean on him, and acknowledge him, his path becomes clear. God doesn't bless "our" path. He blesses "his" path, reveals it to us, and invites us to walk on it.

Do not be wise in your own eyes — It's as if the writer says, "I'm not sure you got what I just said, so I'm going to say it again. Listen up! Don't lean on your own understanding... *don't be wise in your own eyes.*"

Fear the Lord and shun evil — This passage concludes with a challenge to "fear the Lord." Fear in this context doesn't mean being scared. The word "fear" here means to revere God, his wisdom, and his ways. To "shun evil" means to avoid anything that could potentially drive a wedge between us and God. Proverbs 16:6 shows us a direct link between fearing God and shunning evil: "Through love and faithfulness sin is atoned for; through the fear of the Lord evil is avoided."

One of the best examples in Scripture of somebody who trusted God is Job. Job was a wealthy man who lost *everything* — sheep, possessions, children, even his health — even though he was faithful to God. In fact, if Job answered our "Trust God Gap" question, he might have asked, "What does it mean to trust God when you lose it all?" When he lost everything, like many of us, he started asking, *"Why?* Why did I not perish at birth, and die as I came from the womb?" (Job 3:11). And you think *you're* having a bad day!

Yet, despite everything that happened to Job, what was said of him in the very first verse of his book remained true of him throughout his entire life: "In the land of Uz there lived a man whose name was Job. This man was blameless and upright; he feared God and shunned evil" (Job 1:1).

Job came to the realization that knowing God is better than having answers to all of his questions. In the end, God restored Job and made him twice as prosperous as before. When Job faced his own Trust God Gap, his response was ultimately to fear God and shun evil. We could interpret Proverbs 3:5–7 to mean:

> **Job came to the realization that knowing God is better than having answers to all of his questions.**

Submit your heart in full obedience to God. Don't prop yourself up with human wisdom and understanding. In every area of your life, acknowledge God and act according to his wisdom, and he will make the right path — his path — clear to you. Don't be wise according to your own wisdom. Instead, revere God and his ways, and avoid every kind of evil and sin.

What a powerful description of trust. Is it easy? Of course not! It also doesn't mean we're never tempted to revert back to our natural way of thinking. So what do we do when we face our own "Trust God Gap?"

How to Respond to Your "Trust God Gap"

According to Proverbs 3, our response to the Trust God Gap is clear: To trust is to *acknowledge* then *act*. Let that sink in: *to trust is to acknowledge **then** act.*

Sometimes we reverse that order: we *act **then** acknowledge*. We act in our own wisdom, and then acknowledge that we messed up, seeking God's forgiveness and redemption. Other times we act, and then acknowledge God by asking him to bless our action. True trust doesn't reverse the process. True trust begins by acknowledging God, his wisdom, and his ways, and then choosing to act on what we've acknowledged.

To acknowledge God without acting on his wisdom is nothing more than arrogant lip service. To act without acknowledging God is nothing more than self-reliant trust.

To trust is to acknowledge then act.

So, what does it mean to trust God with whatever you wrote in your blank? When you "acknowledge then act," you put *trust* in your Trust God Gap. *Acknowledging* God and his Wisdom and then *acting* on God's Ways is how we ultimately close the gap.

Again, this isn't easy. I [Karen] can see God at work and still have this unsettled feeling inside. *"When's the other shoe going to drop?"* chips away at my mind like a woodpecker pecking a tree. Trusting God doesn't mean you understand it. In fact, that's exactly when you need trust the most... when you *don't* understand. When life doesn't make sense, when life disrupts your plans. But if we don't trust God, we rob ourselves of victories. Testimonies are only experienced on the other side of trust.

A few weeks after Stephen returned home from the hospital, the medical bills started pouring in. We're fortunate enough to have great health insurance, and without it, we would have been financially decimated by the nearly quarter-million-dollar tab. But on April 25th, we were shocked to receive the news that the insurance would only pay a small portion of the nearly $22,000 CareFlite bill. Six minutes in the air came with a hefty price tag.

I called Stephen from work to tell him. "Honey," I said with hesitation in my voice, "I logged on to the insurance's website today. They didn't cover much of the CareFlite bill." I carefully explained that we still owed nearly $18,000. He was speechless.

That afternoon Stephen emailed our business office and asked if they could explore whether or not there might be a mistake — or even an oversight — with the insurance coverage. That night we discussed what to do about the bill. We could ask CareFlite to put us on monthly payments until the bill was paid in full. We could plead our case and tell them that Dr. Parrish ordered the flight, and insist it was a dire emergency.

The scenarios seemed endless as we wondered what to do. While our natural minds had concocted all sorts of scenarios and "what if's", the Holy Spirit whispered just one word to my heart: pray. Our Trust God Gap had grown wider, and prayer was the only way we were going to close it.

My mind was immediately drawn to a point Mark Batterson makes in his book, *The Circle Maker*. Mark challenges us to pray bold prayers and to expect God to surprise us in unexpected ways. He said, "If you want God to surprise you, you have to give up control. You will lose a measure of predictability, but you will begin to see God move in uncontrollable ways."[1] Give up control? Not so easy! But isn't that what trusting God is really all about?

I shared this insight with Stephen, then I grabbed his hand, mustered all the faith that was left in my emotionally depleted soul, and prayed this one simple prayer with him: "God, we take our hands off this situation. Surprise us with your goodness."

In the days that followed, Stephen and our insurance agent talked with our insurance company who kindly, yet firmly, advised us that they wouldn't pay any more of the bill. Then they called CareFlite. They informed us that they had resubmitted the bill to the insurance company, and insisted that they should cover more of the expense. Stephen was cautiously optimistic as he called me to tell me the news. We continued to ask God to surprise us.

On June 4th, we got our final answer. I logged on to our insurance company's website again, this time for an unrelated issue. Suddenly I noticed the "You May Owe" box had a different amount than before. I scrolled down the page, and there it was: God's surprise. Our insurance had paid all but $1,517 of the CareFlite bill. Only God!

> **Why is it so hard for us to trust a God whose track record of faithfulness is flawless? He knows our needs before we ask, and yet he invites us to ask him anyway. Even while we're still praying, he's already gift-wrapping an answer for us in the paper of surprise.**

Why is it so hard for us to trust a God whose track record of faithfulness is flawless? He knows our needs before we ask, and yet he invites us to ask him anyway. Even while we're still praying, he's already gift-wrapping an answer for us in the paper of surprise. That's the God you and I serve. He takes delight in answering our prayers. Trust Him!

Building Trust on Truth

In both of our experiences, certain Scriptures have bolstered our ability to trust God. During those moments of discouragement and setback, God used truth from His Word to encourage, strengthen, and sustain us.

For me [Stephen] that process began before my crisis ever hit. On March 12th, four days before my heart failure, my mom sent me a message: "Stephen, I feel impressed to have you read this chapter in Jeremiah one. I am sure you are familiar with it, but it will be an encouragement to you." While my mom is a very spiritually minded person, she doesn't normally send me Scriptures like this. The very last verse of Jeremiah 1 says, "'They will fight against you but will not overcome you, for I am with you and will rescue you,' declares the Lord."

> **Pre-crisis truth had built my trust in advance, preparing my heart for the actual moment of crisis.**

I can't tell you how many times I thought of that Scripture while I was in the hospital. Although our circumstances were very difficult, I had this overwhelming peace throughout that everything would be okay. Pre-crisis truth had built my trust in advance, preparing my heart for the actual moment of crisis.

On another occasion, my friend Jason visited me in the hospital. While he sat by my side, he asked me, "Is there anything you'd like me to read to you?" I asked him to read me Philippians 1:1–6:

Paul and Timothy, both of us committed servants of Christ Jesus, write this letter to all the followers of Jesus in Philippi, pastors and ministers included. We greet you with the grace and peace that comes from God our Father and our Master, Jesus Christ. Every time you cross my mind, I break out in exclamations of thanks to God. Each exclamation is a trigger to prayer. I find myself praying for you with a glad heart. I am so pleased that you have continued on in this with us, believing and proclaiming God's Message, from the day you heard it right up to the present. There has never been the slightest doubt in my mind that the God who started this great work in you would keep at it and bring it to a flourishing finish on the very day Christ Jesus appears. (MSG)

Those final words in particular deeply encouraged me. God started a work in me, and he had plans to bring it "to a flourishing finish." His plan wasn't done. The apostle Paul's words infused strength into my ability to trust God, even as I was lying there in a hospital bed.

Perhaps one of my most memorable trust-building moments came from two friends, Shawn and Michelle, and their kids Natalyn and Cason, who brought me a very special plaque. (You can read Michelle's personal profile story after chapter seven.) After a warm greeting, Michelle explained the significance of the plaque during her own battle with breast cancer.

The summer before Michelle was diagnosed, their daughter Natalyn went on a mission trip. During the trip, a woman gave Natalyn a rubber bracelet that said, "I can do all things through Christ who gives me strength" (Philippians 4:13). Little did Natalyn know just how much she would lean on that Scripture when her mom received the doctor's report.

After the diagnosis, Natalyn gave the bracelet to her mom to encourage her faith. Weeks later, Michelle shared the story with some friends at her "Pink" party. Some time later, a friend who heard their story gave Michelle a plaque with the same Scripture on it.

Michelle's friend told her, "I believe I need to give this to you. It was a constant reminder and encouragement to me after I lost my 16-year-old son in an ATV accident." She also told her, "Now, when you don't need it anymore, or whenever you feel led to give it to someone else, pass it on." Michelle handed me her plaque and said, "During this process, I felt God wanted me to give it to you." Now I'm the third recipient. And when the time is right, I'll pass it on to somebody else. Again, truth built my trust.

After I returned home, another friend told me she was praying Proverbs 11:25 over me: "A generous person will prosper; whoever refreshes others will be refreshed." She reminded me that I had been generous with others, and her prayer was that God would refresh me as I healed. The very next day, another friend posted this same passage of Scripture on a social media site. God was using two different people — who don't even know each other — to speak the same truth into my Trust God Gap.

After I [Karen] was robbed, fear was the toughest emotion I had to deal with. It bothered me every day that my security had been stolen. Psalm 91 got me through it. That passage begins, "Whoever dwells in the shelter of the Most High will rest in the shadow of the Almighty. I will say of the Lord, 'He is my refuge and my fortress, my God, in whom I trust'" (v. 2–3). Not only were these words a constant reminder of where I should place my trust, but they also reminded me where I could find my rest. Verse 5 was also comforting: "You will not fear the terror of night, nor the arrow that flies by day." Darkness was particularly unsettling for me, I think because the robbery had happened at night. I was reminded that God still stood with me even when the sun disappeared from the sky.

Then there were verses 9–10: "If you say, 'The Lord is my refuge,' and you make the Most High your dwelling, no harm will overtake you, no disaster will come near your tent." This was another promise that I could cling to. God himself is my refuge. Disaster doesn't happen in his tent. Finally, the chapter concludes with these comforting words: "'Because he loves me,' says the Lord, 'I will rescue him; I will protect him, for he acknowledges my name. He will call on me, and I will answer him; I will be with him in trouble, I will deliver him and honor him. With long life I will satisfy him and show him my salvation.'" (Verses 14–16)

In the years following my storm, another passage of Scripture became an anchor for my life. Isaiah 32:18 says, "My people will live in a peaceful neighborhood — in safe houses, in quiet gardens" (MSG). It should be pretty obvious how this verse was able to speak life to into my insecure world. Once again, this was a promise I could hold onto after my plans were disrupted by the unexpected.

> "My people will live in a peaceful neighborhood – in safe houses, in quiet gardens." Isaiah 32.18 (MSG)

You can't build trust on unstable things. Trust needs a firm foundation, or it will crumble with every crack of insecurity. God's Word is the greatest source for building trust. It's fully reliable. It's a fountain of constant comfort, wisdom, and support. It's not just a book of stories, some kind of historical account of men and women who just happened to be used by God. It's a redemptive story. It's living. It's active.

Takeaway #2

The second takeaway when life disrupts your plans is clear: **Trust God by *acknowledging* him and *acting* on his wisdom.** It's easy to say we trust God when life is going our way. It's even easier for us to tell others to trust God. But the true test only happens when life falls apart. When our Trust God Gap is magnified, we discover how much we really do (or don't) trust him.

If your plans have been sidetracked, God is calling you to trust him more. Maybe you like security, like I do [Karen], or perhaps you like plans and strategies like Stephen does. Or maybe you have your own nemesis that puts action ahead of acknowledgement. When the things that matter to you most, or the things that you take for granted, begin slipping through your hands, who do you trust?

The longer I live, the more I realize that all of life is really a journey toward greater trust. God designed it that way. When I've taken a step toward trust, God invites me to take another. When I trust him with my money, he wants to know if I'll also trust him with my time. When I trust him with my career, he wants to know if I'll also trust him with my family. When I trust him with my relationships, he wants to know if I'll also trust him with my emotions. Every step toward trust in God reveals yet another step forward that I can take. That's life. That's what following Jesus is about: how much do I trust him?

When fear knocks at your door, take a deep breath, and replace the question mark with a period. Remind yourself of Proverbs 3:5–7. These words are just as relevant today as they were thousands of years ago:

"Trust in the Lord with all your heart and lean not on your own understanding; in all your ways acknowledge him, and he will make your paths straight. Do not be wise in your own eyes; fear the Lord and shun evil."

A Prayer of Trust

Heavenly Father,
I don't understand everything that is happening to me,
but today I choose to place my trust in you. I surrender my life
fully to your Lordship and to your control. Cleanse me of my sin. Restore
my broken soul. I confess you as my Lord. Help me to acknowledge
you, and then to act according to your wisdom and your will,
in every circumstance I face. Help me to close my "Trust
God Gap," replace my questions with a period, build my
trust on your Truth, and lean fully on you.
In Jesus' name I pray, amen.

PERSONAL PROFILE
Jonathan Holcomb's Story:
A Disruption Named "Loss"

In the spring of 1992, I turned eight years old. As an eight year old, you don't have too many expectations in life. School, friends, sports (specifically Kentucky basketball), and church pretty much defined my world (and my schedule). And while each of these had specific seasons, my family was the one constant in my life. Family was the "thing" that I never had to worry about. Unlike changing weather, Mom and Dad were the unchanging anchor in mine and my older brother's predictably comfortable life.

My dad worked at Lexmark, and my mom stayed at home, her full attention devoted to raising two healthy boys. My brother and I had one job: "go to school." We were raised in a Christ-centered home where

Christianity defined us. It wasn't some list of rules, but rather a genuine way of life.

"Normal" for me was defined by home-cooked meals, T-ball and basketball in the backyard, and enjoying time with my family. I recognize now that my normal, even in the 1990's, was not everyone else's normal. I was very blessed.

Then came winter.

I don't often talk about that fateful day in 1992, when "unexpected" came crashing into my innocent world. While it's hard to find the words to capture the traumatic event that changed the course of my life, it's not uncomfortable to talk about it.

It was the week of Thanksgiving. My dad came home from a run and walked into our 1980's-style kitchen, where he suddenly collapsed on the linoleum floor. My brother, who was eleven at the time, raced down the street to ask a neighbor, who was a lifeguard, for help. Our neighbor ran to our house and immediately started CPR on my dad while we anxiously waited for the ambulance to arrive.

At the hospital, my mom received the devastating news: Dad had had a massive heart attack and died.

Suddenly I found myself in a new, unexpected normal.

Winter would become my new normal. The emptiness, brokenness, and scattered fragments of my life felt like the cold wind on a dark winter's night. It wasn't fair. How would I pick up the pieces? Would spring ever come again?

I've been asked many times how an eight-year old copes with the loss of his dad. I'm afraid my answer doesn't offer much insight at first: "You don't cope… you just live *through* it." I recently heard an analogy that really made sense to me, and I think sheds light on the idea of *living through it.*

All of us have relationship-shaped holes in our hearts. Each hole is uniquely shaped to be filled by an equally unique person: a mom, a dad, siblings… even God. But when one of those relationships is absent from our lives, the other relationships can't fill the void. In my case, my mother did an incredible job raising me and my brother, and yet she was not designed to be a father. She couldn't fill the void that was reserved for my dad. It wouldn't be fair for me to expect my mom — or anybody — to fill the dad-shaped hole in my heart.

What I can tell you is that the pain of losing my dad is no longer pain, but wishful "what ifs." I long for the missed opportunities of sharing my life with the only one who could have filled the void of my dad, David Holcomb. But despite the absence, and regardless of how big that other void might feel, my Heavenly Father is very present. His peace and his presence is my new constant comfort. His blessings have never been more clear to me. I have come to realize that death was never the plan of God, because God is the God of life. I think the apostle Paul expressed it best:

> *And I am convinced that nothing can ever separate us from God's love. Neither death nor life, neither angels nor demons, neither our fears for today nor our worries about tomorrow — not even the powers of hell can separate us from God's love. No power in the sky above or in the earth below — indeed, nothing in all creation will ever be able to separate us from the love of God that is revealed in Christ Jesus our Lord. (Romans 8:38–39, NLT)*

I've found my hope by placing my trust in Christ and his love, not to fill the unique void of the loss of my father, but to fill the unique void in my soul that only Christ can fill. Healing from pain and loss has far less to do with getting rid of pain and much more to do with discovering the hope that redeems our pain. Christ is that hope.

Sin's presence has filled our world with brokenness. We're surrounded by it. It's even in our DNA. But healing has come in the shape of Christ. He fills the voids of our lives with his healing presence. And healing is ours if we'll surrender to him. You can't *take* him; you can only *receive* him.

God also brought other godly men into my life who poured wisdom into the voids I was feeling — voids that had become calloused with fear, anger, and disappointment. But again, my healing — and your healing — starts with surrender. Don't even try to navigate your pain alone; I can tell you, it's not worth it. Instead, run to Christ, where hope will come alive again. By surrendering your life to Christ's comforting strength, choosing to trust him over your pain, you'll begin to heal. Because of his strength, my fears began to subside, and my anger and disappointments began to dwindle. That was when my life moved forward, out of winter and into the new life of spring. The same can happen for you in the middle of your unexpected disruption. *Trust him.* Spring is waiting for you.

CHAPTER 5
Perspective:
Refined or Defined?

Every disruption in our lives is marked by pain, discomfort, or a setback. Pain may be physical, emotional, or mental. Other pain is marked by financial setback or relational collapse. Pain is the temperature that exposes the severity of the crisis.

My [Karen] experience with the robbery was filled with pain. While I wasn't raped or beaten, the emotional pain was deeper than I could have ever imagined. Nobody can predict how they'll respond when their world is shaken by the unexpected. Until the unexpected makes a not-so-welcome visit, everyone speculates what they might do. But it's not until pain takes center stage that you're forced to choose your response.

Response usually brings to mind some kind of action, but during my journey, I discovered the temptation to sink into inaction. Pain has a way of crippling you — not just physically, but mentally and emotionally, too. It has a strange way of paralyzing forward movement and thrusting you into a pit of despair. Many times you don't know what to do to reverse the momentum of your life. Why? Because before you can do it, you have to see it.

Owning It

I was taken aback after the robbery. I'm not sure what I expected to happen, but whatever it was, that wasn't what happened. I quickly discovered that most people don't know what to say to you after something traumatic has happened to you. Most fear saying the wrong thing, so they just don't say anything. Or worse, they say something awkward. Nervousness disconnects their head from their tongue, or they simply treat your pain like the elephant in the room that nobody talks about. But the elephant was crushing my mind and my emotions. My pain became private. I felt isolated. After those first few days, much of my support system outside of my family fell strangely silent.

Everyone else's lives returned to normal, but mine was anything but. I felt like I was shouldering the pain alone, and the mental blame game began sabotaging my mind:

"Don't they understand what I've been through?"

"Can't they see how difficult this is?"

"Do they even care that my whole world has been turned upside down?"

Again, silence. Conversations were often short. Nobody wanted to surface the pain, and as a result, the pain started putting down roots inside of me.

After several weeks, it finally dawned on me: if I'm going to get better, I have to *own* my healing. It was nobody else's job. If I didn't fight through the pain, it would destroy me. Back then, access to counseling wasn't as readily available as it is today. I had to *want* healing enough to do what I didn't feel like doing.

You also have to "own it" if you're the *cause* of your pain. You can't blame "it" on somebody else when you're the reason "it" showed up in the first place. You have to take full responsibility for poor choices, painful comments, bad attitudes, illegal actions, unethical missteps, immoral behavior, and destructive habits. As long as you play the blame game, carefully crafting excuses, or masterfully avoiding responsibility, you'll never recover from your disruptions. In fact, they'll only get worse. John Maxwell often says, "It's easier to go from failure to success than it is excuses to success." Own it! Today!

When you're walking through a crisis, the journey often takes longer than you expect. I had to recognize that it's okay not to heal overnight. At the same time, I knew I couldn't keep living in this dungeon for twenty years. Again,

Sometimes the greatest testimony is found in the struggle. Sometimes the long-term process of healing brings more glory to God than the short-term miracle of healing.

I had to own it. I had to do the hard work or healing wouldn't be possible. Does God heal? Yes! Can he heal in an instant? He can, and sometimes he does. But sometimes the greatest testimony is found in the struggle. Sometimes the long-term process of healing brings more glory to God than the short-term miracle of healing. That was the road I had to travel. The only way to win it was to own it. And the only way to own it was to change my perspective of it.

Perspective Refines Instead of Defines

Perspective is one of the most difficult things to maintain when you're walking through a major disruption. It's hard to maintain perspective when the rocks that keep falling from the sky look bigger by the second. I [Stephen] have often heard that perspective is what separates great leaders from good leaders. I believe that's true for all of us. In fact, perspective is usually the distinguishing difference in how people walk through pain.

In 2 Kings 5 we read about Naaman, a successful commander of the army of the king of Aram. Naaman was highly regarded for his military accomplishments, but his leprosy overshadowed his legacy. Being a leper was feared in Naaman's day because it usually meant suffering, rejection, and isolation. Naaman lived in Syria, a pagan nation north of Israel. His life changed when his path intersected with a young girl taken captive from Israel. We pick up his story in 2 Kings 5:1–3:

> *Now Naaman was commander of the army of the king of Aram. He was a great man in the sight of his master and highly regarded, because through him the Lord had given victory to Aram. He was a valiant soldier, but he had leprosy. Now bands of raiders from Aram had gone out and had taken captive a young girl from Israel, and she served Naaman's wife. She said to her mistress, "If only my master would see the prophet who is in Samaria! He would cure him of his leprosy."*

This Israelite girl is nameless in the story, but from her life we learn a couple of lessons about perspective. Here's the first lesson: my circumstances don't *define* me; they *refine* me for a bigger purpose.

Try to imagine yourself in this girl's shoes. She's a slave, which means she has no rights. She's at the bottom of the social ladder. She's a Jew living in Syria, meaning she's captive in a foreign land. She's young and powerless, especially compared to someone like Naaman. And she's a female in a very male-dominated culture. If that were you, how would you respond?

While many people might take a low view of themselves in this situation, this young, nameless girl's perspective was greater than her circumstances. Her identity was established in her God, not in what was happening around her or to her. That's the second lesson we can learn about perspective: your identity must be defined by *who*, not *what*.

If you let WHAT (your circumstances) define your identity, then your identity will change every time your circumstances do. Crisis will be your middle name. But if you let WHO (Jesus Christ) define your identity, then your identity will not change because Christ is unchanging.

Our society has a completely different message. In our culture today, identity is usually defined by two things: opinions and circumstances. Most of us struggled with opinions when we were in junior high and high school. What people thought of us was almost more important than breathing. For many people, that constant search for approval followed them into adulthood. So why is that a problem? Because when you own people's opinions of you, they own your future.

Other people allow circumstances to define them. They feel trapped in the prison of the present, and they can't see past the here and now. As a result, their identity is synonymous with their circumstances.

So who defines you? Are you defined by opinions and circumstances, or do you find your identity in Christ? Does the direction of your life change with the wind because your identity is tied to whatever's happening around you (whether good or bad)? If you can settle this identity issue, then you can start seeing your circumstances as an opportunity to refine you, not define you. And that's just what this servant girl did.

2 Kings 5:2b–3 tells us, "…she served Naaman's wife. She said to her mistress, 'If only my master would see the prophet who is in Samaria! He would cure him of his leprosy.'" Although this girl was captured, taken to a foreign land, and forced into slavery, still she let her circumstances *refine* her, rather than *define* her. How? In two ways.

First, she *served*. That's the last thing any of us would want to do if we were taken captive in a foreign land. You might say, "Well, of course she served. She had no other choice." That's true, but *how* did she serve? That is seen in her second response.

The servant girl served with *sympathy*. She had compassion for her master by suggesting that he go and see the prophet Elisha in hopes that he would be healed. The girl not only *served*, but her heart was filled with sympathy for her master. Just because she knew about Elisha — and even suspected he might be able to heal Naaman — she didn't have to say anything. In fact, she could have kept that information to herself out of spite for her situation. But because she chose instead to be sympathetic, she didn't keep quiet as her master experienced suffering, rejection, and isolation. She chose to offer hope to Naaman, by telling him about a prophet who could heal him. How could she do this? Perspective! Her circumstances didn't define her, but they refined her for a bigger purpose.

So what was the bigger purpose? As we read the rest of this story, we discover that Naaman took the girl's advice, and he was healed. But something even greater happened. 2 Kings 5:15 says, "Then Naaman and all his attendants went back to the man of God. He stood before him and said, 'Now I know that there is no God in all the world except in Israel. So please accept a gift from your servant.'" God's bigger purpose for Naaman was that his heart (and the hearts of all his attendants) be turned toward God.

When you're in tune with God's bigger purpose, you'll let your circumstances refine you instead of define you. It's when you lose sight of God's bigger purpose that you become bitter at your circumstances. Viktor Frankl is a great example of someone who maintained perspective in extraordinarily difficult times.

> **When you're in tune with God's bigger purpose, you'll let your circumstances refine you instead of define you.**

Viktor showed an interest in psychiatry while growing up, and at the age of 25 he became a successful medical doctor in Vienna. He married Tilly Grosser in 1941, but in 1942, they were arrested by the Nazis. They were forced to abort their child and were transported to the Theresienstadt Ghetto, in what is today the Czech Republic.

After spending three years in various concentration camps, Viktor was finally liberated, along with others in the camps, on April 27, 1945. But after returning to Vienna, he discovered that his wife, mother, and brother had all died.

Most people in Viktor's situation would allow their circumstances to define them. And you probably wouldn't blame them after having suffered such terrible abuse. But Viktor's incredible perspective enabled him to respond differently. During his lifetime, he wrote thirty-nine books, received twenty-nine honorary doctorates, and taught at four universities. His book, *Man's Search for Meaning*, which he dictated in only nine days in 1946, had sold nine million copies by the time he died in 1997.

> **Everything can be taken from a man but one thing: the last of the human freedoms – to choose one's attitude in any given set of circumstances, to choose one's own way." – Viktor Frankl**

One quote from *Man's Search for Meaning* powerfully describes Viktor Frankl's perspective: "Everything can be taken from a man but one thing: the last of the human freedoms — to choose one's attitude in any given set of circumstances, to choose one's own way."

Imagine having this kind of perspective in your crisis. Imagine how you would view your circumstances differently. Imagine how you would respond to tests, trials, and the ups and downs of your disruption. Your circumstances don't have to define you. But with the right perspective, they can refine you.

Look at Me

You may be familiar with the saying, "You either have big PROBLEMS and a little god or little problems and a big GOD." It's all a matter of perspective. While it's an easy thing to say, of course it's a much harder thing to live.

Moses understood the overwhelming feeling of despair and inadequacy when God called him to lead the children of Israel out of Egyptian bondage. In Exodus 6:29–30, God addresses Moses, saying, "I am God. Tell Pharaoh king of Egypt everything I say to you." But Moses, full of fear and insecurity, shot right back, "Look at me. I stutter. Why would Pharaoh listen to me?" (MSG)

Have you ever felt that way? God prompts you to do something, and your immediate, default response is to remind God of all of the reasons why his idea is such a bad one? Shaking your head, you say, "Look at me!" You do your best to draw God's attention to everything that's wrong with you... your lack of talent, resources, skill, and good looks.

I love God's response to Moses. When Moses says, "Look at me..." God doesn't waste a minute. He fires right back: "Look at *me*" (Exodus 7:1, MSG, emphasis mine). Then He tells Moses:

I'll make you as a god to Pharaoh and your brother Aaron will be your prophet. You are to speak everything I command you, and your brother Aaron will tell it to Pharaoh. Then he will release the Israelites from his land. At the same time I am going to put Pharaoh's back up and follow it up by filling Egypt with signs and wonders. Pharaoh is not going to listen to you, but I will have my way against Egypt and bring out my soldiers, my people the Israelites, from Egypt by mighty acts of judgment. The Egyptians will realize that I am God when I step in and take the Israelites out of their country (Exodus 7:1–5, MSG).

God knows how to put things in perspective. When we're crying, "Look at me," God is quick to shoot back, "No! You look at me." You can't put your disruptions in perspective until you take your eyes off your disruptions and put them squarely on God. Then you'll understand how God responds to your problems. The next time you're tempted to wallow in your insecurities, your inadequacies, your inabilities, your inferiority, step into the shadow of God instead. Be reminded of how big God really is. Let God's still, small voice speak those three big words to you: "Look at me."

Emotional God

When we face a crisis, it's easy to get myopic and lose perspective. It's easy to stand paralyzed in the shadow of the problem. And it's easy to feel like God has abandoned you, leaving you to face your problems alone. Disruptions are emotional. They highlight our pain so much that we allow them to hide our God. That's why it's so important to accept God's invitation to "Look at me."

Because disruptions are emotional, it's also important to understand the emotional side of God. God doesn't stand on the sidelines, some kind of cold, heartless deity with zero interest in our crises, trials, and challenges. In his sovereignty, he listens, remembers, and sees. And he understands.

This response is evident in Exodus when the children of Israel were in Egyptian bondage. The Israelites were groaning and crying out for relief from their hard labor. In Exodus 2:24–25 we read God's response to this overwhelming pain. Notice how deeply God was moved by the Israelites' problem:

"God **LISTENED** to their groanings.
God **REMEMBERED** his covenant with Abraham, with Isaac, and with Jacob.
God **SAW** what was going on with Israel.
God **UNDERSTOOD**" (MSG, emphasis mine)

Isn't that what all of us are looking for when we face a crisis? God's response isn't restricted to Bible times. He still LISTENS, REMEMBERS, SEES, and UNDERSTANDS. As you stand toe to toe with the unexpected, don't forget the posture God has assumed right alongside of you. He's *listening* to your cry for help and *remembering* His promises to you; he *sees* every detail of your problem, and he *understands* what you need in your darkest hour. If that's how God responds to you during your crisis, run *to* him rather than *away* from him. Don't let your pain overshadow the emotional side of God.

A New Perspective

The book of James was one of the earliest written books of the New Testament. James was a respected leader of the church in Jerusalem, dealing with some of the most practical issues of everyday life. Some people consider the book of James to be the Proverbs of the New Testament. While the issues in James are *common challenges*, James offers us *uncommon wisdom*.

His letter begins with this challenge: "Consider it a sheer gift, friends, when tests and challenges come at you from all sides. You know that under pressure, your faith-life is forced into the open and shows its true colors. So don't try to get out of anything prematurely. Let it do its work so you become mature and well-developed, not deficient in any way" (James 1:2–4, MSG).

In James' day, the problem faced by the church was persecution for their faith in Christ. Straight out of the gate, James tackles this problem without apology. Does he tell these early believers that God will comfort them in their problems? No! Does he offer encouraging words to those facing the fear of death? Nope! Does he speak words of affirmation, hope, or peace? Not one word! Instead, James begins, "Consider it a sheer gift, friends, when tests and challenges come at you from all sides."

The truth about problems is that we often *add* a problem to our problems. As if the cake wasn't big enough already, we finish it off with a layer of problematic icing called "problematic perspective." Perspective makes all the difference in how we view and respond to problems. In fact, without the right perspective, we live with a terminal case of problematic nearsightedness. But with the right perspective, everything can change.

> **Without the right perspective, we live with a terminal case of problematic nearsightedness. But with the right perspective, everything can change.**

I don't know about you, but James' advice on how to view problems is not my *natural* response to the problems I face. I don't usually see problems as a *"sheer gift."* But James understood an important reality about problems that we need to embrace today: problems work *for* us, not against us. James helps us see that the problems we face in life do two things for us.

First, problems *reveal* our character. James said, "…You know that under pressure, your faith-life is forced into the open and shows its true colors." Second, problems *refine* our character. James continues, "…So don't try to get out of anything prematurely. Let it do its work so you become mature and well-developed, not deficient in any way."

In his book, *In a Pit with a Lion on a Snowy Day*, Mark Batterson shares the story of Nazi concentration camp survivor Corrie Ten Boom. After surviving the camps, Corrie Ten Boom spoke to audiences about her horrific experiences. As she would speak, she always looked down… but not at her notes. She was working on a piece of needlepoint.

After sharing about the pain and anger of her experience, Corrie would hold up the needlepoint for her audience to see. First, she would show them the back of the needlepoint, a jumbled mess of threads, and say, "This is how we see our lives." Then she would show the audience the design on the other side and conclude with these words: "This is how God views your life. And someday we will have the privilege of viewing it from His point of view."[2]

Corrie could have questioned why she had to suffer in Nazi concentration camps. It didn't make sense. It was unfair. Instead, she gained perspective that enabled her to grow into a person that she otherwise would never have become. She didn't let her disruption disrupt her perspective.

Every pain in your life is either a teacher or a master. If you let your pain serve you as a teacher, then you'll learn lessons from your pain that you

> **Every pain in your life is either a teacher or a master.**

can leverage for your future. But if you instead allow your pain to become your master, you'll be its slave. It will dictate your life and swallow your future without apology. Corrie Ten Boom chose to make pain her teacher, not her master, by adopting the proper perspective of her pain. So can you.

Perspective is Followed by Action

After my surgery, my recovery process was slow. I like progress, so it was unsettling when my recovery took weeks and months... rather than days. Ironically, the sermon I preached to conclude the "Winning the War Within" series on the day of my heart failure addressed the fruit of the Spirit. I even shared an illustration about *patience*. What I had preached was now being put to the test.

My perspective had to change. I had to see things differently, and I had to do things I didn't want to do. After a surgery, you don't want to do anything that causes more pain. You want to lie in bed and sleep. Rest is essential, but so is activity. The more your body moves, the faster your body heals.

When I could barely feed myself, the nurse wouldn't let Karen help me. "He's old enough to feed himself," she insisted. The first time I had to walk, I wanted to hide under the covers of comfort in my bed. It was painful. Watching me walk was slower than waiting for Christmas. My steps could literally be measured in inches.

The ICU nurse told Karen, "He's going to need lots of encouragement." From that moment on, whether I was walking, eating, or doing the simplest task, Karen and Ashley would tell me, "You've got this." That became their new mantra. I heard them say it dozens of times. Those three little words were an anthem out of Ephesians 6:10: "Finally, be strong in the Lord and in his mighty power."

When I returned home, I had to breathe every hour using a spirometer. That was the only way to ensure my lungs would open up enough to continue fighting off infection. I'd set an alarm on my phone to remind me. I was tempted to just sit there in my chair, reclining all day. But the more the body moves, the faster it heals. I had to do what I didn't want to do. I had to think differently, see differently, then act differently.

Takeaway #3

The fact that you're reading this book means you're probably dealing with some sort of unexpected disruption in your life. At the very least, you're wondering how you can navigate the problems you're facing each day. Our third takeaway for how to handle disruptions is perhaps one of the most important: **Choose to see what others can't see, so you can be what others won't be.**

Having the right perspective is a choice. It doesn't come naturally. It fights every emotion inside of you. It calls you to do what you don't want to do. However, without the proper perspective, you'll always strike out. You'll

Perspective is like a gateway to everything God wants to do in and through you during (and after) your disruption.

never be what you could be. In fact, without perspective, you won't embrace any of the takeaways in this book. Perspective is like a gateway to everything God wants to do in and through you during (and after) your disruption.

When you choose to see what others can't see, you set yourself up for greater personal growth. You become what others won't be. In other words, you make the hard choice that so many others avoid. When they reject perspective, what they're actually rejecting is future growth. Choose to see what others can — or won't — see. When you do, you lay a foundation for God to work. Above all, you allow God to pull the good out of the bad.

A Prayer for Perspective

Heavenly Father,
It's so hard to see straight when problems mount in my life.
Today, I choose to fix my eyes on you. Help me to rest in the reality
that you listen to my cries, you remember your covenant, you see my
situation, and you understand what I'm feeling. Above all, help
me to allow my circumstances to refine me, not define me.
Give me the strength to own my healing and the courage
to own my failures. Help me to see what others can't see,
so that I can become all that you've called me to be.
In Jesus' name I pray, amen.

CHAPTER 6
Family:
Care, Compassion, and Conversations

R egret is powerful, like a voice from the past yelling at you through a megaphone into the present. Unfortunately, most people go to their grave with regret haunting them. Too often those regrets are tied to relationships, especially with our families.

As I lay in the hospital, I can honestly say that regrets — especially relationship regrets — weren't hanging over my head. There were no phone calls seeking forgiveness to be made. There wasn't a need for hard conversations to smooth over past hurts. I love my family, and I'm grateful for each one of

Regret is powerful, like a voice from the past yelling at you through a megaphone into the present.

them. During this journey, they played a crucial role, and I was reminded of the treasure found in family.

Get to Fort Worth

When my parents [this is Karen] heard of the robbery, they were on a road trip to Tennessee to see the foliage change of the beautiful trees. They were shocked when they heard the news, and they immediately got on the road to return home. When they finally arrived, my dad had to peel his fingers off the steering wheel. The stress of the situation made him tense during the entire drive home. He and Mom had only one quest: get to Fort Worth to see their daughter. As I recovered emotionally, they also demonstrated wonderful care and understanding. They never made me feel ashamed when I didn't want to stay alone. They patiently walked with me throughout the healing process.

My situation was similar [this is Stephen]. As the news about my condition worsened, Karen kept my parents, brothers, and sister aware of everything that was happening. At the time, Mom and Dad were in California visiting my sister Nikki. My older brother Chris was on a business trip, and my younger brother Mike was working locally. Initially, when we thought I had pneumonia, my parents asked if they should head home. Karen said she'd keep them posted as we got more information. As the seriousness of the situation became apparent, everyone scrambled to get to Fort Worth. That's how much they cared.

Mom later told me they were devastated. When Dad heard the news, he cried, fearing the worst. The thought of losing a child was too much to bear. When they had left town on Saturday, I was in perfect health. Now, two days later, everything had changed. Mom said, "It stabs your heart. It's worse to lose a child than a spouse because you expect your kids to outlive you."

Miraculously, my parents were able to book an early morning flight (with exactly three seats available, so Nikki was also able to join them). At four o'clock Tuesday morning, Eric (Nikki's husband) got them to the airport in record time so they could catch their 6:20 flight. They didn't think they'd make it in time for my surgery, which was originally scheduled for 10:30 am. But because a surgery before mine went long, mine ended up being delayed.

Unlike most flights, they arrived at Dallas/Fort Worth twenty minutes early, where Chris's wife Ruth picked them up and brought them to the hospital. When they arrived, the waiting room was filled with people. Chris, already back from his business trip, was there to welcome Mom, Dad, and Nikki with open arms. When he brought them to my room and Mom saw me connected to all of those tubes and wires, she immediately burst into tears. Of course, I was still intubated, so I didn't even know they were there.

All of them prayed for me together. Mom especially has a gift of prayer. They pleaded with God to restore my health and to guide a successful surgery. Just as they were saying "Amen," the operating team arrived to wheel me into surgery. The timing of the events surrounding everyone's rush to Fort Worth before my surgery is nothing short of amazing.

The Compassion of Family

Each member of my family showed me tremendous compassion, but each one did so in different ways. Even though Mom and Dad were upset, they remained hopeful in prayer. Mike worked quietly behind the scenes, even setting up a funding opportunity to help us pay for some of my medical expenses. Nikki never stopped encouraging my parents and my family. She kept telling Mom, "I completely believe Stephen's going to be all right." Her confidence reminded mom of the Scripture she had sent me a few days earlier: "'They will fight against you but will not overcome you, for I am with you and will rescue you,' declares the Lord" (Jeremiah 1:19).

Chris was like an anchor. He has a unique gift for humor and a sharp mind, which came in handy for asking doctors all the right questions to get as much information as possible. He stood by Karen's side, constantly encouraging and stabilizing her. When the worst had passed, he started joking around to help everybody lighten up. Shawn and Michelle, friends who walked with Karen through the toughest hours, gave her a journal where our friends and family could write their thoughts and encouragement.

Chris wrote, "First, you really went overboard to get your own personal helicopter ride — you know you can just hire a charter over DFW! On another note, I have now been charged with giving you a nickname based on your new bionic heart — name forthcoming (requires appropriate level of embarrassment, etc.)." When the family gets together, he's the one doing standup comedy. He also wrote: "I hope the ratio of Thomsons [Karen's family] to Blandinos doesn't overwhelm you. You have an awesome support system and people who REALLY love you — including me!" Chris's wife Ruth also shared wonderful words of hope and encouragement, as well a deep gratitude for our family.

Nikki expressed sincere love and compassion, her faith married to a gritty resolve. She wrote: "You are loved by so many, and we want you around for longer than the rest of us. Got it?" I'm still waiting to get my nickname from Chris, but in the meantime, I'm keeping the one Mike gave me: "Ironman." His wife Jessie wrote the lyrics to a worship song that affirms how awesome God is, about how willing he is to heal and to strengthen.

Mom and Dad both expressed their love for me as any parent who takes pride in their children. Mom wrote, "Our love for you is unending… we are all continuing to pray and believe God for your continued and complete healing." Dad wrote: "You are secure in his Word, and your path has been chosen. Be at peace in this knowledge. I love you, Stephen."

I didn't get to read the whole thing until I finally got home from the hospital. As I did, tears filled my eyes. Ashley's words were perhaps the most encouraging. When a child expresses their sincere and genuine faith, that does something inside a dad. She wrote, "God is so good, and it's times like this when we truly see that. …We can't wait to tell you all the crazy miracles God has provided."

Karen's family was also extremely supportive and encouraging. They spent literally days in the waiting room. They prayed, encouraged, and supported us in so many ways. Roy and Pearla [Karen's parents] affirmed God's big picture purpose for my life, and Bo and Jessica [Karen's brother and sister-in-law] shared their love and support (and chocolate chip cookies!).

Every family member said, "I love you!" — probably the most important words I could hear, soothing my soul and bringing me assurance and comfort. Perhaps the greatest expression of love was when Dad prayed for me.

Dad's Prayer

I had been moved from ICU to a regular room, and the day was coming to an end. Mom, Dad, Chris, and Ruth all gathered around me to pray before heading home for the night. After a couple of them prayed, Mom turned to Dad and said, "Sal, why don't you pray for Stephen?"

You have to understand: while my dad is strong in his faith, he's quiet about it. It's very personal to him. He prays, but he doesn't enjoy praying out loud. He's never felt adequate or equipped to pray publicly, so he keeps his prayers quiet and private. Perhaps those are the prayers Jesus honors the most. Jesus actually said, "But when you pray, go into your room, close the door and pray to your Father, who is unseen. Then your Father, who sees what is done in secret, will reward you" (Matthew 6:6). Quiet, simple, sincere. No fanfare. Authentic.

I had never heard my dad pray out loud until that night. And his first audible prayer… was for me. It was more than I could handle. My lip was quivering as he carefully chose each word to lift me up to our Heavenly Father. Hundreds of people prayed for me during that time, but if there was just one prayer I could bottle up and save, it would be Dad's. There's nothing like a son hearing his dad pray for him.

Dinner Conversations

When I returned home, Karen and I had the most intimate conversations of our lives. Many times over dinner we talked about the entire experience. She shared her hopes and fears. She told me what was happening during the time I was intubated. She described the timeline in detail and shared the journal with me. With every conversation, we grew closer together. And with every conversation, we both experienced emotional healing.

Now, we've always had a good marriage, but this experience did something I can't really explain in words. The depth of love that Karen showed me was like nothing I've ever known before. The way she served me, cared for me — just genuinely loved me — has been simply extraordinary. It was true, unconditional love.

Takeaway #4

We don't know the condition of your family relationships. As a pastor [Stephen], and as a counselor [Karen], we're smart enough to know that there are hundreds of dynamics that shape families today. Many people have been abused. Others carry deep-rooted hurts from earlier years. There's a good chance somebody even owes you an apology. Although you may not realize it, there may even be somebody out there waiting for an apology from you, too.

> **Family is too important to go through life with a grudge against the ones who should love you the most. Relinquish regret before it's too late.**

All we can say is this: grudges aren't worth it in the long run. That brings us to our fourth takeaway for navigating disruptions: **Relinquish regret and relate to, or restore, your family.**

Family is too important to go through life with a grudge against the ones who should love you the most. Relinquish regret before it's too late. Reach out and make things right. If they don't reciprocate, it's okay. You've done what you can do. In this life, we will have trouble. Storms will come. As much as it depends on you, do everything in your power to ensure that your family will be standing by your side when those storms roll in.

A Prayer for Family

Heavenly Father,
Thank you for my family. Regardless of who has hurt me,
or who has brought me happiness, help me to express Christ's love to
each member of my family. Today I choose to relinquish regrets,
restore any broken relationships, and build healthy relationships
with my family. I choose to forgive those who have hurt me,
and to extend forgiveness to those I have hurt.
Thank you for the gift of a loving family,
and thank you for the gift to
love unconditionally.
In Jesus' name I pray, amen.

CHAPTER 7
Community:
Sequoia Trees, Waiting Rooms, and the Power of Love

When I [Stephen] talk to people about the power of community, I often like to tell the story of the great Sequoia trees. These giant trees, the tallest on earth, live to be more than 2,000 years old! Reaching heights of nearly 380 feet, these enormous species tower over all of nature.

The Sequoia National Park has 8,000 of these impressive trees, including the General Sherman Tree, a single, massive Sequoia with a circumference of over 100 feet and an estimated weight of 2.7 million pounds.

It's hard to look at large trees like the Sequoias without almost immediately wondering what must be going on with their roots. For a tree to be so tall, its roots would have to be equally impressive in depth, right? How else could they stand? But that's actually not the case with Sequoias. Their roots are usually no more than five or six feet beneath the surface, yet they grow up to 100 feet in length from the base of the tree.

So what's the secret to the Sequoia's ability to stand? These extraordinary trees only grow in groves, with their roots intertwining with the roots of other Sequoias. When storm winds blow, the trees remain standing because the winds aren't fighting just against the strength of one tree at a time; they're fighting against the entire grove.

> **Most of us can't withstand the storms of life by ourselves. But everything changes when we put down our roots in community with other followers of Christ.**

Real community works like that. Most of us can't withstand the storms of life by ourselves. But everything changes when we put down our roots in community with other followers of Christ. The strength of our community stands against the winds of the storm because the community's roots are fused together.

I've been involved in small groups for years. Prior to planting 7 City Church, I served as an executive pastor, where part of my responsibility included leading our small group ministry. Before that experience, small groups were not a big part of my life.

All of that changed in the years leading up to the launch of 7 City. We led several small groups in our home, forming great friendships with people both inside and outside the church. I didn't realize it at the time, but that one adjustment made an extraordinary difference when major disruption entered our lives.

Waiting Room Bonding

When Stephen was in the ICU, the response from family and friends was simply overwhelming. Sixty-seven people gathered in the waiting room during those first couple of days. At one point, I counted ten people standing in his ICU room (which of course he was oblivious to). In fact, after his surgery, Stephen's nurses had to put their foot down.

Two of the friends who came during that time were Shawn and Michelle. Stephen and I had the great privilege of walking with them through their own crisis in the previous year when Michelle was diagnosed with breast cancer (you can read Michelle's personal profile after this chapter). Now here they were, walking by our sides.

Shawn was one of the first people to hear that Stephen was sick. He texted Stephen that Monday morning and asked if he was coming to the men's small group at our church. Stephen texted back, "I'm sick. Klen's leading today." As the day progressed, so did the severity of the text messages I sent to Shawn and Michelle (and a host of other friends).

That day, Michelle raced to the hospital as Stephen was being transported by helicopter. She met another friend, Jennifer, and together they awaited Stephen's arrival. Ashley and I were driving, and by the time we arrived, Michelle and Jennifer were already there to meet us. I immediately broke down. "Stephen is my compass. I don't know what I would do without him," I said. They comforted me as the darkest hours were approaching.

The only way I know how to describe what was happening in the waiting room is what I guess I'd call "waiting room bonding." There were so many people and so many emotions. Chris entertained pockets of people with his offbeat sense of humor. Others were engaged in serious conversation. And, of course, unanswered questions floated through everyone's minds like dense clouds hanging in the sky.

Amidst the questions and emotions, friends and family, even those who didn't know each other, were bonding. It was a beautiful picture of community. Genuine love. Sincere compassion. Hopeful anticipation.

Shawn left work Monday to head to the hospital. Before coming, he called Michelle to see if she (or anyone else) wanted anything to eat. That was a dangerous offer to make to a room full of hungry people. Within minutes, Michelle was taking In-N-Out Burger orders for nine people in the waiting room. When Shawn placed his order at In-N-Out, the young man at the register asked him, "You going to a party?"

Shawn thought, *I **wish** it was a party.*

After arriving at the hospital and distributing everyone's food, Shawn and Michelle went into the ICU. Stephen and Shawn had grown closer as friends during the previous couple of years. Between the challenges with Michelle's cancer diagnosis and Stephen's efforts to disciple Shawn (personally and with a small group of guys), they had developed a solid friendship.

When they walked into Stephen's room and saw him intubated, Shawn was suddenly speechless. He later admitted that Stephen had become such a pillar of strength in his life that seeing him helpless like that was just too much for him to bear. As they were praying for Stephen, he had a coughing fit, a common occurrence with the condition of his lungs. Shawn and Michelle were visibly shaken as the nurses began tending to his care. They struggled to regain their composure before heading back into the waiting room where I was sitting.

When they came back to us, Shawn walked over to Klen and Derek, who were talking on a nearby couch in the waiting room. Shawn was trying to be strong, but he suddenly broke. Derek consoled him. Reflecting on that moment, Shawn made a wonderful observation: "Having the right people, in the right place, at the right time, made the difference." That's the power of community.

When you don't know what to do, community stands in the gap with you. When you don't have answers and all your security evaporates, community is the anchor you hold on to. And when your immediate future is darkened by an overwhelming disruption, community is who you lean on.

> **When you don't know what to do, community stands in the gap with you. When you don't have answers and all your security evaporates, community is the anchor you hold on to.**

Community Cares

Your community is made up of people who genuinely care. Michelle was looking out for both of us. She later told us, "Everybody took a different role. One role was to protect Karen and Ashley. They needed to see the confidence in our eyes that everything was going to be okay." Michelle even befriended the nurses. One day she showed up with a dozen tiny Bundt cakes for people in the waiting room, and a separate dozen for the nurses. When she delivered them to the nursing staff she told them, "These are for y'all. Please take good care of Stephen."

While standing in the ICU room, I'll never forget Derek leaning over to whisper something to Stephen. Stephen, of course, wasn't aware of his surroundings, but that didn't stop Derek. Derek whispered to him, "You're going to make it. We believe that. God's got plans for you." And that remained his stance the entire time. Derek had an unshakeable peace that everything would be fine, and he chose to speak life into Stephen's spirit.

During this entire ordeal, I had to learn to embrace community at an entirely different level. I don't like to burden people, so my reflex reaction is to tell people I'm okay. But I wasn't. In situations like this, you pray for God to give you a peace like a cocoon. But the truth is, there are just too many ups and downs. You can't get out of it by yourself. You need others to help you. Without community, the healing process is longer and more difficult. When Stephen's heart failed, I knew I couldn't walk alone.

The "others" we leaned on were deep and wide. I remember turning to a pastor friend and saying, "I think we'll need someone to cover the pulpit for a couple of weeks." "A couple of weeks" turned into six... including Easter Sunday. And our associate, Klen Kuruvilla, took the lead in this church that was only eighteen months old. He and his wife Audrey were like a rock, loyal and devoted, as Stephen recovered. They sat in the waiting room for hours and even brought practical gifts — expressions of compassion and love. When Klen wrote in Stephen's journal, he signed it with, "Holding your arms" (Exodus 17:11–13). And truly he did.

At home, the support continued. Numerous friends brought meals every night for more than two weeks. Michelle and Jennifer decorated the house for Stephen's birthday before he returned home from the hospital. Cards, flowers, and fruit arrangements flowed in regularly. Another friend took care of our lawn. People visited and offered incredible words of encouragement. I thought I understood community before, but now I truly do. Why would you ever want to do life alone?

Community: A Place to Belong and Become

All of us were born into the global family of human beings. But God also designed us to *belong* to a specific family... a place where we find nurture, care, love, and safety.

This same principle is true with our spiritual family—the family of God. 1 Peter 1:3 says, "All honor to God, the God and Father of our Lord Jesus Christ; for it is his boundless mercy that has given us the privilege of being born again so that we are now members of God's own family. Now we live in the hope of eternal life because Christ rose again from the dead" (TLB). Author and pastor Rick Warren says, "You become a part of the human family by your first birth, but you become a member of God's family by your second birth."[3]

> **Community is the place where you belong and become.**

So what happens in our spiritual family? Being rooted in relationships with other Christ followers empowers an extraordinary process of community. A foundational truth is at work here: community is the place where you *belong* and *become*.

Sociologists suggest that our society is experiencing what they call "crowded loneliness." Author Randy Frazee wrote, "The 'hard to swallow' premise is that today's church is not a community but rather a collection of individuals."[4]

We can find meaning only in the context of our relationships with the family of God. In Romans 12, the apostle Paul makes a comparison between our physical bodies and the family of God. He writes: "In this way we are like the various parts of a human body. Each part gets its meaning from the body as a whole, not the other way around. The body we're talking about is Christ's body of chosen people. Each of us finds our meaning and function as a part of his body. But as a chopped-off finger or cut-off toe we wouldn't amount to much, would we?" (Romans 12:4–5, MSG)

According to Paul's instruction, the organs in your body find their purpose and meaning only when they're connected to your body. If your heart, lungs, or kidneys were removed from your body, they wouldn't have any meaning or function. That's what the body of Christ is like. We find meaning when we're connected to Christ's body… to his family.

Unfortunately, some followers of Christ don't think the church (the family of God) is necessary. In fact, some people don't even *like* the church — much less *love* it. They seem proud to say inflammatory things like, "I love Jesus, but I hate the church." But there's a problem with statements like that: the Bible calls the church "The Bride of Christ" and "The Body of Christ." How can you love the Head but hate the body? As Rick Warren observes, that would be like me saying, "I love you, but I dislike your wife."[5]

> **Pain caused by the body of Christ is not a license to cut off the body of Christ.**

You might say, "But you don't know how other Christians have hurt me." And you'd be right. I don't know. But I do know this: pain caused by the body of Christ is not a license to cut off the body of Christ. Even when the rocks are thrown by other Christians, we don't have the luxury of alienating ourselves from Christian community. Ephesians 2:19 says, "Now you are no longer strangers to God and foreigners to heaven, but you are members of God's very own family, citizens of God's country, and you belong in God's household with every other Christian" (TLB).

When we receive Christ, we belong to the *global* family of God. Obviously, it can be difficult to feel like you're part of a family with billions of members. So what does God call us to do? He calls us to be involved in the *local* family of God… the local church. Even then, it's still easy to hide in an auditorium where we sit in rows of strangers to sing songs and listen to a speaker talking about God's Word.

No, to truly belong, we must connect with a small group of people where we can experience community. Acts 2:46 says, "They worshiped together regularly at the Temple each day, *met in small groups in homes for communion, and shared their meals with great joy and thankfulness*" (TLB, emphasis mine).

The early church understood that for people to truly belong, they have to engage in a smaller environment where they can be known. Regardless of your personality type — whether you're an extrovert or introvert — every one of us needs community. And not only do we need community, we need it frequently.

Community is a place where we belong. It's a place where we can be known. But community is also a place where we *become*. Ephesians 4:15–16 says, "Instead, speaking the truth in love, we will grow to become in every respect the mature body of him who is the head, that is, Christ. From him the whole body, joined and held together by every supporting ligament, grows and builds itself up in love, as each part does its work."

To "become" means growing into the person that God intended us to be. Again, that happens best in the context of community. Community is a place to belong *and* a place to become.

When the apostle Paul wrote his letter to the church in Philippi, he challenged followers of Christ to press on toward the goal of knowing Christ. He even warned them to avoid people who might distract them from this goal. Paul wrote: "Stick with me, friends. Keep track of those you see running this same course, headed for this same goal. There are many out there taking other paths, choosing other goals, and trying to get you to go along with them. I've warned you of them many times; sadly, I'm having to do it again. All they want is easy street. They hate Christ's Cross. But easy street is a dead-end street. Those who live there make their bellies their gods; belches are their praise; all they can think of is their appetites" (Philippians 3:17–19, MSG).

Paul understood that avoiding "dead-end friends" would have a direct bearing on our growth. Author and pastor Rob Ketterling made a powerful observation that I believe captures the essence of Paul's words. He said, "Our relational circle has an effect on the direction and speed of our lives."[6]

The right people will direct you in the right direction, but the wrong people will direct you in the wrong direction. It's not like this is rocket science. Paul said, "Do not be misled: 'Bad company corrupts good character'" (1 Corinthians 15:33). Ketterling observes that "bad company" actually refers to two things: *bad people* and *bad teaching*. In other words, the people you hang out with and the teaching you expose yourself to will lead your life in a specific direction. They can lead you down a dead-end street or drive you toward health and growth. Solomon said, "Walk with the wise and become wise; associate with fools and get in trouble" (Proverbs 13:20, NLT).

Your closest relationships are not only like a compass in your life, they're like the gas pedal too. They'll determine the direction of your life, and they'll help you get there faster… for good or bad.

Psychologist Ed Diener made an interesting observation about the happiest people. He discovered that the differentiating factor in their lives was *high-quality* social relationships. Social psychologist Dr. David McClelland, from Harvard University, calls the group of people with whom you habitually associate your "reference group." According to his research, your "reference group" determines as much as 95% of your success or failure in life.

Charles "Tremendous" Jones highlighted this truth when he said, "You are the same today that you are going to be in five years from now except for two things: the people you associate with and the books you read." And Jim Rohn said, "We are the combined average of the five people we hang around the most." Both men understood the direct impact people have on the direction and speed of your life.

If you don't like your life, look around you. Who are your friends? They may be helping you go farther, faster — but what direction are they taking you? Show me your friends, and I'll show you your future. Proverbs 12:26 says, "The righteous choose their friends carefully, but the way of the wicked leads them astray." All friends push you farther, faster. Pay attention to which direction they're pushing you. If they're not going in the direction you want to go, find people who are, and make friends with them. Engage in community with other Christ followers. They'll provide a place to belong and become.

> "We are the combined average of the five people we hang around the most." – Jim Rohn

Known by Love

I [Stephen] have never known how deep love can go as much as I have during and after my heart failure. Throughout this entire process, I was reminded of a passage of Scripture from the Gospel of John. Jesus said, "By this everyone will know that you are my disciples, if you love one another" (John 13:35).

Notice that Jesus wasn't referring to their love for unbelievers. Obviously that also needs to be a priority in our lives, but in this passage, Jesus is referring to the disciples' love for one another. Love between fellow Christ followers communicates a loud message to our world. People pay attention to how we treat one another.

I've thought many times, *What would people who don't follow Christ think if they knew how much love I've been shown since my heart failure? How attractive would Christian community be to the world if they knew the depth of love expressed in such an environment?* These thoughts challenge me. They stretch me. They push me to love well. How well are we known by love?

Takeaway #5

The fifth takeaway when life disrupts your plans is this: **Cultivate community before, during, and after the storm.** Cultivating community before the storm means *investing* in relationships. Cultivating community during the storm means *leaning* on those relationships. And cultivating community after the storm means *serving* those relationships.

You might not think you need community. Maybe you're convinced that your life is just fine without it. Perhaps you're even scared of what community might cost you. We're here to tell you that community is worth every deposit of time, energy, and emotion. You may not need to make a withdrawal today, but one day, you will. And when that time comes, the question's going to be answered: has your community account been building interest all this time, or did you never even open it?" Choose wisely. Choose to start now.

A Prayer for Community

Heavenly Father,
Thank you for the amazing support of loving friends.
Thank you that I don't have to walk through my storms, setbacks,
and sins alone. Today I choose to live in community with others.
Please bring friends into my life who will love me unconditionally.
Enable me to be a true friend who invests in relationships
and selflessly serves others. Help me to let down my
guard and lean on others in my time of need.
In Jesus' name I pray, amen.

PERSONAL PROFILE
Michelle Yates' Story:
A Disruption Named "Cancer"

"You have cancer."

I don't think anyone or any thing can prepare you for the moment when your doctor shares that painful diagnosis with you. I turned forty in February 2012, and I had my first mammogram in August of that year. Within a week of that mammogram, I received the phone call every woman dreads. The breast center called to schedule me for a *second* mammogram and sonogram. They had found an irregularity in my screening.

The second sonogram confirmed their suspicions. "Oh honey, this is not your friend," my technician said. "What?" I was in shock. The next day I had a biopsy that would confirm that I had invasive ductile carcinoma: breast cancer. My husband, Shawn, was out of town when I received the news. I had to tell him about it over the phone. As we discussed what we were going to do, we decided we would be completely honest and forthcoming with our children about my diagnosis. At the time, our daughter Natalyn was twelve, and our son Cason was eight.

When we told our kids, Natalyn got up and went to her room. A few moments later she returned with a black plastic bracelet. Natalyn had been on a mission trip earlier that summer to Ruidoso, New Mexico. She began to tell us that one day a lady approached her and handed her this bracelet. "I believe you will be needing this soon" the woman had told her.

Inscribed on the bracelet were these words: "Philippians 4:13 I CAN DO ALL THINGS THROUGH CHRIST WHO GIVES ME STRENGTH."

Shawn and I just sat there and cried. Even before any of us knew what was about to happen, God had placed this woman in my daughter's path to let us know that he was in control.

During the month before my surgery, God continually put that scripture in front of me. My friend Cathy had lost her teenage son in an ATV accident years before. I had always admired her as a pillar of grace and strength, and our friendship grew even closer after my diagnosis. During a "Pink" party that a couple of my friends threw for me, Cathy gave me a plaque with Philippians 4:13 inscribed on it. She told me that after her son Sean died, she found herself in a very dark place in her life. One of her friends gave her this plaque as a gentle reminder of where her peace and strength ultimately comes from. Knowing that I was facing a journey that would require that same peace and strength, she gave the plaque to me. I had never felt so humbled, so honored.

In October 2012, I had a double mastectomy, and in November I began chemotherapy treatments. When you're a woman, and you lose everything that defines you in society as a woman — your hair, your eyelashes, your eyebrows, and of course, your breasts — it alters how you feel about yourself. I felt like my identity had been stolen from me. Where I had once been a strong, confident, independent woman, I had been reduced to an introverted, self-conscious, dependent mess. On the outside — to my friends and family — I put on a brave smile and toughed my way through what I knew I could conquer. But inside? Deep inside I struggled with emotions I had never felt before.

I constantly worried about whether my husband would find me attractive anymore. I could hardly look at myself in a mirror, let alone let him see me. The devil worked very hard to tear our family apart. The months that followed my diagnosis were like an emotional rollercoaster, filled with unexpected twists and turns. But every time I was at my lowest, feeling like I was trapped in the valley of the shadow of death, God in his infinite wisdom would send just the right person into my path to lift me up. I suddenly found myself surrounded by a community of people who truly cared about me. Sometimes it was as simple as a text message or a short prayer. Other times it was a meal, a card, a call, or a visit. And sometimes it was the warm embrace of a hug from a friend or a family member.

Each member in my community of friends had a gift... one that 1 Corinthians 12 describes as a *spiritual* gift imparted by the Holy Spirit to his church. Each person's gift reveals who God is, and each gift serves a unique purpose. In those darkest moments when my emotional tank was depleted and my physical strength was gone, God would prompt one of his children to unwrap their gift and bless me — or my family — with it. And because they listened and obeyed, we found the strength to make it through this difficult journey.

You never know how you're going to respond to a disruption in your life until one unexpectedly shows up. For me, I decided to fight. My fight required strength, but the truth is, it wasn't really me who was strong. It was *Christ in me*. And when the enemy flexed his strength to destroy me, or my relationships, God's strength was always greater. His mercy and his wisdom never ceased. And when I felt like I couldn't fight any longer, my community of friends and family would rally around me to fight on my behalf.

The things you learn during a crisis like this mark you for the rest of your life. One of the most poignant discoveries I found was how important your God-given gifts are. You really do play a unique role in this life, one that the Author of Life has custom crafted just for you. When you choose to step into your assignment, God uses not only your gifts, but your experiences as well, to reveal his Glory, to advance his Kingdom, and to make a difference in the lives of others.

My journey through breast cancer left not only physical scars on the surface that others could see, but it also left emotional scars below the surface. But Christ is faithful. He constantly reminds me of his love. He faithfully places friends and family in my path who encourage me, pray for me, and walk this journey hand in hand with me. My scars are a regular minder of the faithful God that I serve. He hasn't forgotten me. He hasn't forsaken me. He hasn't abandoned me. Neither has the community that I get to do life together with.

CHAPTER 8

Purpose:
Leveraging What Is for What Could Be

Several years ago I [Stephen] was at a conference where I heard pastor and author Craig Groeschel say, "If you're not dead, God's not done." I was reminded of this again when I awoke from surgery and learned just how close I had come.

Several conversations reiterated this truth deep in my soul. My cardiologist told me, "God must have something left for you to do." Other friends and family said similar things. My good friend Derek wrote in my journal: "During the last two days, we have prayed, cried, prayed, and prayed. The whole time I knew all would be well. I knew this because God has so much left for you to do. There are more books to write, blogs to post, and cities to influence."

In the earlier years of my leadership, my good friend Steve Moore taught me about the importance of something he called "destiny markers." A destiny marker is an event or circumstance from the past that gives you clues to your purpose in the future. God carefully sows these seeds of destiny as a way to reinforce and recalibrate our lives to his divine purpose. They're reminders of God's sovereign plan to use us for his glory. Purpose is more than a matter of the present or the future; its origins began before you ever even asked the question, "Why am I here?" Our job is to leverage what is (our pain, destiny markers, and gifting) for what could be (our divine purpose).

Nothing reveals this truth to me more than another verse from that passage of Scripture my mom sent me just days before my heart failure. Jeremiah 1:5 says, "Before I formed you in the womb I knew you, before you were born I set you apart; I appointed you as a prophet to the nations."

Finding Meaning in the Suffering

Laura Bush once observed that there are some things you expect, and others that you don't, when serving as the First Lady of the United States. In her case, she never expected to become an advocate for the women of Afghanistan. Yet, while the circumstances were unexpected, Laura Bush made her influence count when it was needed the most. She said that you have to "use the things that you didn't want to happen to you in a way that can be constructive."

The same is true for us. All of us have things happen to us that we didn't want — unexpected events — but we have to choose to respond to those things in a way that's constructive. When the rocks of distress and disruption pelt us like hailstones, we have to search for meaning in our suffering. As I mentioned earlier, that's just what Victor Frankl did, the concentration camp survivor and author. In his book *Man's Search for Meaning*, Frankl wrote, "Suffering ceases to be suffering in some way in the moment that it finds a meaning." You may not see it right now, but there's meaning hiding in the shadows of your pain. The very rocks that bruise you hold a nugget of gold inside of them. Go looking for it! God's brewing up a greater purpose that will outlast your pain, but He needs you to open your eyes and see it. The purpose of pain is not to punish you. Instead, regardless of the source, God wants to use your pain to prepare you for a greater purpose. He wants your suffering to find a meaning by allowing Him to redeem your pain.

God's purposes preceded your birth. Before you even arrived on the scene, God had already etched His divine plan into your DNA.

> **When the rocks of distress and disruption pelt us like hailstones, we have to search for meaning in our suffering.**

But God's purposes also preceded your suffering. Just because the unexpected showed up on your doorstep doesn't mean that it aborted God's purpose for your life. So how do you discover that purpose? How do you find meaning in your suffering and discover God's unique plan for your life?

The Four Stages of Life Purpose

"What is God's purpose for my life?" Perhaps no other question has generated more frustration in our culture today. In my experience, the journey toward discovering your life purpose typically includes four distinct stages: *Divine Purpose, Designed Person, Discovery Process,* and *Devoted Pursuit.*

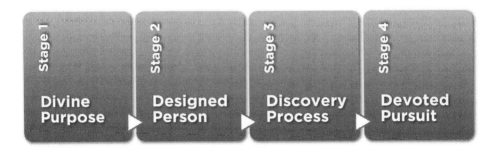

Stage One: Divine Purpose — Our journey began when God created each of us for a Divine Purpose. Paul called that purpose "good works" in Ephesians 2:10: "For we are God's handiwork, created in Christ Jesus to do good works, which God prepared in advance for us to do." This is a verse rich with destiny. In God's wisdom, he created us with our purpose already in his mind. He defined "good works" for us in advance. In other words, God began with our purpose. Even if some of us were surprises (at least to our parents), none of us were accidents. Purpose preceded the creation of you.

Stage Two: Designed Person — Because God started with our divine purpose, he uniquely designed us to fulfill that purpose. Not only did God create us for good works, but He also equipped us for those good works. That means that he deposited within us a unique design — our gifts, abilities, personality, and passions — to fulfill our God-given mission.

Stage Three: Discovery Process — The Discovery Process is usually where we experience either frustration or fulfillment. We search for answers, we pray for direction, we seek counsel. Many people spend their entire lives in the discovery process. Unfortunately, many people (most?) even go to the grave never having satisfied their longing for purpose. They die before they discover.

Stage Four: Devoted Pursuit — When the discovery process finally begins to yield some answers, then we're faced with the ultimate question: "Now that I know this purpose, am I willing to pursue it with full devotion?" Stage four is where all of us want to live. It's the place we dream of in our search to matter. It's also the place where God holds us accountable for our understanding of our purpose.

When we're navigating the stages of life purpose, most of us tend to ask one obvious question more than any other: "What's my purpose?" While there's certainly nothing wrong with that question, often it can leave you feeling like you're wandering aimlessly. Rather than focusing solely on purpose (the first box), look carefully at design (the second box). In other words, don't just ask, "What is my purpose?" Also ask, "How did God design me?" Your answers to the second question will provide context and direction for the answer to your first question.

Discovering Your Design

If God designed you with your purpose in mind, then you owe it to yourself (and to God) to learn as much as possible about how God designed you. Ask yourself these questions to get started:

- What are my natural abilities and skills?
- What are my spiritual gifts?
- What kind of personality do I have?
- What am I most passionate about?
- What are my hopes and dreams for the future?
- What needs in the world do I feel compelled to meet?
- What problems in the world do I feel drawn to solve?

- What audience or group of people do I feel called to serve?

- What can my past successes and failures reveal about my strengths and passions?

- When a book, sermon, speech, article, event, or activity ignites my interest, what is the subject matter?

- What seeds (circumstances, relationships, events) has God sown in my past that might offer clues to my purpose for the future?

- How do I sense God leading me right now?

Your answers to these questions reveal how God uniquely wired you. They provide evidence toward your God-given design. As you answer these questions, you'll discover common threads woven through your answers. Those common threads shed light on the "good works" God has called you to do. In other words, your design reveals your destiny.

You're Called

So many people get caught up in the rat race of a career that they end up disconnecting themselves from God's purpose. We're so busy comparing ourselves to other people (and then trying to get ahead of them) that we feel destined to die without ever discovering our true calling.

In the church world, pastors often promote a sincere (yet misguided) view that to be "called into the ministry" is the highest way a person can serve God. In fact, if you ever went to church camp as a teenager, you might even have heard a speaker offer an altar call for people who felt "called." So here's my question: How come these speakers rarely or never gave an "invitation" for people who were called to serve God in business, media, education, politics — or any other channel of culture?

Let's be honest. Most pastors would probably say, "Well, sure God calls people to be in business. How else would he fund his Kingdom?" While certainly I agree that business leaders can positively impact the financial needs of church work, I would also suggest that that view is extremely shortsighted. Calling is about much more than funding someone else's "ministry."

Millions of believers live with a misinformed worldview that divides the spiritual realm from the physical realm. This ancient Greek dichotomy of "sacred" vs. "secular" isn't even biblical. Worse, it presents a skewed interpretation of Scripture. Instead, man is called to redeem *all* of culture, what Chuck Colson and Nancy Pearcey called "The Cultural Commission."[7] The cultural commission is all about shaping culture under Christ's lordship. It's allowing God's purposes to shape every channel of culture over which we have influence.

Os Hillman, author of *The 9 to 5 Window*, observes that of Jesus' 132 public appearances, all but ten were in the marketplace, while forty-five of His fifty-two parables had a workplace context. In the book of Acts, we find forty miracles or divine encounters — thirty-nine of which occurred in the workplace![8]

> "'The priesthood of all believers' did not make everyone into church workers; rather, it turned every kind of work into a sacred calling." – Gene Edwards Veith, Jr.

Here's the point we want you to get here: when leaders restrict "calling" to just the church world, they diminish the biblical idea of calling and remove the power of the Gospel to redeem the marketplace and culture. Calling isn't just for pastors — YOU are called. Gene Edward Veith, Jr. once wrote, "'The priesthood of all believers' did not make everyone into church workers; rather, it turned every kind of work into a sacred calling."[9]

Consider the very term *vocation*. Vocation comes from the Latin word for "calling." What we consider a job to pay the bills is actually so much more than that. And if you think that business, politics, media, banking, social services, education, engineering, art, or construction isn't a "holy" calling, then who (or what) makes the call sacred? The call is sacred because of *who* it comes from, not what it's to. The source of the call, not the function of the call, is what makes the call sacred. A holy God does not produce unholy callings. God has the authority to call anyone he chooses… to whatever vocation he chooses.

> The call is sacred because of who it comes from, not what it's to. The source of the call, not the function of the call, is what makes the call sacred.

The "good works" you do may be different from the good works that I do. But those works — although different — were prepared in advance for *you* to do. *You* were called and created to do them.

Plastic Urinal

One night during my hospital stay, I found myself needing to get the attention of my nurse. It was the middle of the night, and I couldn't find the call button. I patted all around on both sides of my bed, but the clicker was nowhere to be found. The door to my room was cracked, so I tried calling out to her, but I just couldn't get her attention.

Finally, in desperation, I started looking for something I could use to make some noise. All I could find was the plastic urinal container, next to my bed, just at arm's length. I grabbed it and began banging it against the side of the table. (It was empty.) Louder and louder I banged, until finally someone at the nurse's station heard me.

When the nurse came into my room, she was mildly irritated. "Why didn't you just push the call button? That's what it's for, you know."

I assured her I would much rather have simply buzzed her, but I couldn't find my call button anywhere. She sighed, exasperated. "Look. It's right here!" She reached where it should have been, but when she couldn't find it "right here," she too began frantically searching around for it. Finally she found it, tucked well out of my reach. She untangled it and put everything back where it should have been, setting the controller back beside me.

Trading Your Career for a Calling

Most of the nurses who took care of me at the hospital were extremely helpful. Each one of them had their own personality, but each one also genuinely served. In fact, there was really only one exception, and yes, it just so happened to be the nurse whose attention I had to get with the plastic urinal.

For whatever reason, this particular nurse could never seem to get things quite right. She was often in a rush, she didn't ask questions, and she left things undone. Multiple times I had to buzz her (when the buzzer was in reach) to ask her to close my door, turn off a light, help with medications… the list went on. One night while I was lying in bed, it suddenly occurred to me what the difference was between her and everyone else who was taking care of me. Her job was just that… a J-O-B. It was a paycheck. She didn't seem to have a sense that she was called. Consequently, excellence didn't really matter to her.

Unlike this one nurse, others had traded their career for a calling.

Deb was one such example. Deb worked the night shift. During her first shift with me as a patient, she told me as she was leaving the room, almost as an afterthought, "Oh, and I pray for all my patients." With that, she closed the door. Over the next couple of nights, she was meticulous in her attention to detail. Deb was gentle, kind, and compassionate. She was constantly popping in to ask if there was anything I needed. I rarely had to buzz her because she got things right the first time.

Here's what was most amazing about Deb: even as she was taking such great care of me, she was going through her own crisis. Her husband had recently left her, and her mother had recently passed away. Yet, despite her own world of unexpected disruptions, Deb saw her job as a calling. She served sincerely and with excellence. My last night in the hospital, it was my birthday. That night, Deb brought me a birthday card that she and all of the other nurses had signed. Simple gestures of kindness make all the difference in the world. That's the difference between a calling and a career.

Then there was Peggy. Peggy certainly didn't have the highest-paying job on the hospital staff. Part of her responsibility was bathing the patients. If you have a modest bone in your body, you just kind of have to get over it in circumstances like the one I was in. There I was, naked and in pain, getting my first shower in days. I couldn't wash my body or my hair. And yet Peggy served me with kindness and compassion. As I was sitting there, water pouring over my body, I said, "Peggy…"

"Yes?" she asked in her Southern accent.

"I don't know how much money you make. But whatever it is, they should double it." She laughed and smiled. What was a thankless job for many was a calling for this precious lady.

Other nurses offered genuine smiles backed with cordial personalities. One told me about volunteering at her church with a special nursing program. Even my cardiologist told me he was following my progress each day while I was in the hospital — and that he was praying for me to fully recover. Career or calling? When you understand your life purpose, your calling becomes clear, and your life is infused with new passion.

Finding Your Calling in the Mundane

Maybe you feel trapped in your career. You may even have another career in the works, but you're temporarily confined to your current job. It's easy to see a dream job as a calling, but what if it's a lackluster job? How do you find your calling in the mundane? Consider trying these four approaches:

1. **Change your priorities.** What is the twenty percent of your job that you enjoy the most? What part of your job gives you some measure of satisfaction? Identify that part of your job first; then start exploring how you can prioritize more of your time around it. Even if you can't allocate more time to that twenty percent, especially right away, simply identifying it will give you something you can look forward to each day.

2. **Change your posture.** So often we race to our jobs, frazzled by the traffic, the kids, or the fact that we're running late. What would happen if you ordered your morning so you could start work from a posture of peace? Maybe that means arriving fifteen minutes early and praying for your job, your co-workers, and the events of the day. Maybe it's grabbing coffee once a week with a friend who encourages you and prays with you. Simple steps like these allow you to develop a new posture toward your job.

They can help you frame your work with the works God wants to accomplish *through* you.

3. **Change your perspective.** It's so easy to fall prey to the mundane, especially if your co-workers do as little as possible just to get by. Colossians 3:23 says, "Work willingly at whatever you do, as though you were working for the Lord rather than for people" (NLT). Our responsibility as followers of Christ is to do our work with excellence, and to do our work as if God were our boss. If you were working for God, you wouldn't skimp on the quality of your work. When you adopt this perspective, it changes the motivation of your work — and the excellence you deliver on the job.

> **Our responsibility as followers of Christ is to do our work with excellence, and to do our work as if God were our boss.**

4. **Change your position.** Finally, consider how you can transition into a position or a role that better matches your gifts, abilities, and passions. This might require you to return to school, seek additional training, or even apply for a new job. Undoubtedly it will cost you the coziness of your comfort zone. Stop complaining about what is, and start planning for what could be. Your transition plan might also include staying with your current company or organization, but slowly carving out a role that leverages your strengths. When your strengths add value to your company, your leader will take note. This may lead to greater opportunities that are better aligned with your sweet spot.

If you feel trapped in the mundane, you have to change your priorities, change your posture, change your perspective, or change your position. It's possible you'll change all of these. But each change you make can help you focus more on how God equipped you to fulfill your purpose and pursue your calling.

Take Your Next Step

Whatever crisis you find yourself in, it should touch the *life purpose* nerve in your soul. As great as the pain might be, if you're not dead, you're not done. Something should come alive inside of you. Do you need to heal? Yes! Do you need time to reflect on the crisis you've walked through? Absolutely! But your healing and reflection should ultimately drive you further toward your purpose in life.

Taking a step forward with your life purpose typically plays out in two ways. First, your crisis might drive you into a deeper discovery process. This is a wonderful place to be. I [Karen] discovered this firsthand in the years that followed the robbery. After jumping from one job to the next, my purpose finally became clear to me as I took considerable time to reflect on my deepest passions. A sense of urgency arises when you find yourself dissatisfied with your life and in search of greater meaning. If that's you, seek the Lord first and foremost (Matthew 6:33). Be sure you're not trying to satisfy the cravings of your soul with things that are

One of the greatest ways to redeem your crisis is to allow it to thrust you deeper into your purpose. Don't wait for your purpose to happen to you. It's waiting for you on the other side of risk.

apart from God. Furthermore, discover how God has uniquely wired you. Keep peeling back the layers of your life until you discover the "good works" God has called you — and designed you — to pursue.

Second, your disruption might drive you to pursue new roles or opportunities aligned with who God made you to be. Life-altering events often push us to take bigger risks because we realize that we're all running out of time. Some of those risks involve new opportunities, job changes, pursuing a degree, volunteering in our community, or championing a cause we love.

One of the greatest ways to redeem your crisis is to allow it to thrust you deeper into your purpose. Don't wait for your purpose to happen to you. It's waiting for you on the other side of risk. Discover it and pursue it. Find your calling and live fully alive.

I Needed You

"God must have a purpose for your life" is something both of us heard after our disruptions. However, it's also important to understand that God's purpose for your life is bigger than your job, your passions, or your dreams. God's purpose is relational too. When Stephen returned home from the hospital, my heart expressed a different perspective. I told Stephen, "I know God has a purpose for your life. I know He's going to do something great in our future. But *I* also *needed* you."

Your purpose isn't restricted solely to what you do. It also includes those closest to you. Whether you're a spouse, parent, or close friend, your purpose is enriched in relationships. Relationships are significant because people are eternal. You'll retire from your job. Your accomplishments will cease. The contributions you make with your talents and resources will come to an end. But people? People are eternal! The relationships you build, and the investment you make with friends and family, will outlive you. Your purpose is more than profit or productivity; it's a picture of partnership.

Takeaway #6

The sixth takeaway to embrace when life disrupts your plans is powerful: **Discover and pursue God's purpose that will outlast your pain.** Returning to your old routines and worn-out safety nets isn't God's best. Carefully reflect on who you are and on what God wants to do through you. Embrace the richness of relationships, and invest in the eternity of people.

Most of us hate the unexpected. But what if there were a good side to the unexpected? What if the unexpected became the launching pad to a new life, one filled with divine purpose? What if that purpose could outlast your pain? And what if God wanted to use the unexpected to reveal His calling to you? In the Old Testament, that's exactly what happened to Joseph.

As a teenager, God gave Joseph a wonderful dream, but through a series of unexpected events, his dream seemed to derail. His brothers sold him into slavery, he was falsely accused

> **What if the unexpected became the launching pad to a new life, one filled with divine purpose? What if that purpose could outlast your pain?**

of attempted rape, and he languished forgotten in prison. That is, until God's timing for the dream had finally come. Joseph was summoned to meet with the king, and he correctly interpreted the king's dreams. Instantly Joseph went from the prison to the palace. He became the second in command in Egypt.

All of us like instant success. But in between Joseph's dream and Joseph's destiny were thirteen years of unexpected disruptions. There's an old saying: "Most overnight successes are twenty years in the making." Had God forgotten him during this season? Not at all! He was simply preparing Joseph for a dream far bigger than himself. He was forming a purpose that would outlast Joseph's pain.

You may hate the unexpected disruption that you're dealing with right now. But stop and consider Joseph's story. Maybe God is up to something greater. Don't misunderstand: I'm not suggesting that God created your crisis; what I *am* suggesting is that God wants to use that crisis to brew up a greater purpose for you to fulfill. Again, that takes perspective.

That's how Joseph ultimately came to view his series of disruptions. After a famine hit the land and his brothers came looking for food, Joseph's dream was fulfilled. As his brothers knelt before him, Joseph revealed his identity. Needless to say, his brothers were scared to death since they were the very ones who had kicked off Joseph's thirteen years of misery in the first place. But Joseph's ultimate response revealed his maturity: "'Don't be afraid of me. Am I God, that I can punish you? You intended to harm me, but God intended it all for good. He brought me to this position so I could save the lives of many people. No, don't be afraid. I will continue to take care of you and your children.' So he reassured them by speaking kindly to them" (Genesis 50:19–21, NLT).

What a powerful response! Joseph found purpose in his pain. He leveraged what was for what could be. In his words, "God intended it all for good." Joseph didn't let the intensity of his pain overshadow the positive impact that pain could mean for others. I believe the same is true for you. Despite how you feel, and the pain that you're dealing with, if you'll allow Him to, God intends to do something good with it. Calibrate your heart toward God's greater purposes. He's working. Are you listening?

A Prayer of Purpose

Heavenly Father,
Thank you that you have a purpose to fulfill in the midst of my pain.
Today I choose to find the meaning in my suffering. Like Joseph,
redeem my pain and turn it into something beautiful. Help me to
leverage my gifts, abilities, passions, and pain to make life better
for others. Reveal your purpose to me, and empower me
to live for a purpose bigger than myself.
In Jesus' name I pray, amen.

PERSONAL PROFILE
Byron Kauffman's Story:
A Disruption Named "Financial Distress"

I love music! Getting to play my bass in a band was a dream come true during my younger years. So you can imagine how I felt when I launched an audio company with a good friend. We both worked full-time jobs, but we dreamed of the day when it would become a full-time business.

After a few years, my friend decided to get out of the business and move on to other adventures. Not long after we parted on good terms, I changed jobs and received a generous raise. I didn't need the headaches of running a business, so I decided to sell the company to my employee… who eventually defaulted on our sales agreement. That started a downward spiral into a series of unexpected events that would disrupt my life for more than ten years.

The company was tens of thousands of dollars in debt, and I had no choice but to sell the business to a couple of friends for next to nothing. The new owners secured additional contracts throughout the United States. As a result of the company's growth, they were in need of a vehicle capable of pulling an equipment trailer long distances. Neither of them had good credit (which should have been my first warning sign), so they approached me for help. I talked it over with my wife, and then I agreed to lease a Ford Excursion, the largest SUV on the market at the time, under the condition that they would assume the lease as soon as possible.

I've always defaulted to the belief that if you don't have clear direction, you should follow your peace. There was no peace to be found in this situation. And yet, for whatever reason, I conveniently looked the other way while God was trying to get my attention.

As if that wasn't enough, these same guys talked me into leasing a very nice 4x4 truck for my own use. Eventually business tailed off, and I got stuck with making most of the lease payments. So I did what any sensible businessman would do: I let these guys use my truck too, and then I leased myself a new Chevy Blazer. Financial expert Dave Ramsey would have been proud of me! (Byron said, sarcastically.)

Two weeks later, the owners split ways, and I was stuck with nearly $2,000 in monthly lease payments (as well as our personal car payment). The repo man made a visit to my workplace to stake his claim on the 4x4 truck. Embarrassment doesn't even begin to describe what I felt when the security guard called me at my desk. I work in a profession that requires a security clearance, which means that credit issues could have resulted in the loss of my clearance — and therefore my job. I agreed to a voluntary repossession, which cost me $15,000. Doing my best to dig a deeper hole, I put that 15K on my credit card.

And the Excursion? It unexpectedly appeared on my curb one day. What do you do with a vehicle that's a little over a year into a 48-month/80,000 mile lease... with 56,000 miles on it? You keep making payments. I tried to find someone to buy out the lease on the Excursion, but the lease company wouldn't budge. Lease payments went on my credit card, along with the school tuition for our two boys.

Things went from bad to worse. In 2003, I was diagnosed with Chronic Myeloid Leukemia. Hearing "Leukemia" when you're sitting in your doctor's office feels like getting a death sentence. I remember walking out of the doctor's office, sitting in the car, and becoming angrier and angrier. I turned to my wife and told her, "You know what? We're going to beat this." I was adamant in my determination as my mind was filled with gritty resolve.

"You won't have to raise our boys by yourself. In fact, we're going to shove this thing so far up the devil's rear end that he'll choke on it." That might sound kind of radical, but that was how I felt, so that's what I said. My visit with the oncologist two days later turned out to be a positive one. We discovered that the treatment was an extremely expensive (but effective) pill called Gleevec. Thankfully we have great insurance, and the ongoing treatment didn't (and hasn't) set us back financially any further. As bad as things were, one good thing came out of my diagnosis: it took my mind off of our financial pressures.

By 2004, I had paid off the vehicles, but I still had roughly $60,000 in debt on our credit cards. You probably already know this, but your credit score doesn't fare too well when it includes a repo and 120-day late notices. The interest rate on the credit cards climbed, one reaching over 28% on a $20,000 balance. Finally, in the fall of 2013, we paid off the last of the credit cards.

My credit card payments during that 10-year stretch were $1,500 per month. Do you know what it's like to pay $1,500 every month toward your financial mistakes? It's not just a one-time disruption to your life. It's a monthly reminder multiplied by 120 months. That's $180,000! Like clockwork, this monster showed up in our mailbox every thirty days, ready to devour the next payment. I'll never forget feeding this beast for the last time. It was like breaking a yoke off my neck that had bound us for years. And while much of our financial misery was brought on by my poor decisions, it still hurt. Badly. Unexpected disruptions often do.

That said, I was — and still am — pretty hard on myself because of the foolish decisions I made that put my family's well-being into jeopardy. But I can't afford to waste so many years of pain. Reflecting on these disruptions, I've picked up a few lessons along the way.

First, I've never been a big fan of praying for my debts to be miraculously canceled. God sent up plenty of warning signs in advance, but I ignored them (and him). I had to own my failures. Through this process I've discovered the God of second chances, and his gracious wisdom to provide me with a shovel to dig out of my financial hole. Through it all we didn't starve. I didn't lose my security clearance, and I even excelled at work while my salary nearly doubled from 1997 through 2013. Our summer vacations were low-budget, but we still had a good time.

Second, dealing with leukemia helped put things in the rest of my life in perspective. Suddenly I saw life differently, and my financial problems didn't seem to be so bad after all. I was challenged to reorder my priorities, and to recognize what's really most important in life: God.

Family. Even taking the time to celebrate the little things.

Finally, I'm only now able to look toward the future, and how God might want to use the pain that we've endured. I don't have all the answers, but I'm committed to discovering how God can use our disruptions to help others. I refuse to waste over a decade of pain. That's my story of the unexpected, and how God is redeeming it for good.

CHAPTER 9
Legacy:
Write It While You're Living

Andrew Carnegie once said, "There are two types of people who never achieve very much in their lifetimes. One is the person who won't do what they're told to do. The other is the person who does no more than they're told to do." Both of these people abandon their legacy to the realm of insignificance.

You want to leave a legacy worth remembering when you die. The question is, are you writing a legacy worth recording while you're living? Legacy doesn't start when you take

You want to leave a legacy worth remembering when you die. The question is, are you writing a legacy worth recording while you're living?

> **Death is simply the stamp that delivers your legacy – for good or for bad – to future generations.**

your last breath. It starts when you make your first choice. Your daily decisions are the runway of your legacy. Your investments in people today determine what they will remember tomorrow. You choose your legacy every day. Death is simply the stamp that delivers your legacy — for good or for bad — to future generations.

Finishing Well

Something strange happened on the morning of my heart surgery. I blog regularly on the subjects of leadership, personal growth, church, and culture. As with any blogging platform, you can write an article and schedule it to post on your blog on whatever day you choose.

Over the 2013 Christmas break, I spent time writing and refreshing some articles to post in 2014. One of those articles was titled, "Being in the One-Third Who Finish Well." I refreshed the article in early January and then picked a date for it to be published. What day did I pick? Tuesday, March 18th, 2014: the day of my heart surgery.

When I scheduled that article two months earlier, of course I had no idea what would be happening on March 18th. In fact, I had forgotten all about the article. Imagine what my friends and family thought (and felt!) when they saw an article hit their inbox and pop up on their social media, on the topic of "finishing well"... the morning of my surgery. Strange? Ironic? How about downright freaky? Here's a copy of that article:

Leadership professor Bobby Clinton has conducted extensive research revealing that only one-third of leaders finish well. Clinton observes that many of the issues that derail leaders include misuse or abuse of finances, abuse of power, pride, sexual misconduct, unhealthy family relationships, wounding, or a plateau in personal growth.

So what does it take to finish well as a leader? Reflecting on Clinton's research, I would suggest that there are six keys:

1. ***The Right Purpose:*** *Leaders who finish well have a clear sense of destiny and recognize the life purpose for which God created them.*

2. ***The Right Priorities:*** *Leaders understand that balance in key areas of life is essential to finishing strong. These priorities include areas such as intimacy with Christ, family strength, and key responsibilities that contribute to health.*

3. ***The Right People:*** *Finishing well does not happen on an island alone. Leaders embrace a network of coaching and mentoring relationships to help them in the journey. These relationships may be a combination of intensive, occasional, and distant mentors.*

4. ***The Right Plan:*** *Leaders maintain a deep commitment to lifelong learning by developing a plan for personal development. Leaders who finish well recognize that a learning posture is essential for continuous improvement and breaking through growth plateaus.*

5. ***The Right Practices:*** *Leaders who finish well embrace spiritual disciplines and lead by example. They operate from a base of influence shaped by spiritual authority.*

6. ***The Right Parameters:*** *To finish strong requires leaders to establish clear boundaries. These parameters and accountability safeguards help leaders maintain purity and avoid the abuse of people, money, and power.*

The odds are stacked against leaders when it comes to finishing well. But it is possible. Will you be in the one-third who finish strong? Which of the six ingredients above are missing in your life? Which is your greatest strength?

I certainly didn't plan on "finishing" my journey on March 18th, 2014. Obviously God had other plans too. But the fact that my article was published that same day gives me cause to pause and reflect. Are the six keys to finishing well alive and well in my life? You can't decide *when* you finish, but you can determine *how* you finish. Legacy doesn't happen in a day; legacy happens every day.

You can't decide when you finish, but you can determine how you finish. Legacy doesn't happen in a day; legacy happens every day.

The Legacy Pyramid

Author and family ministry leader Reggie Joiner once said, "An inheritance is something you leave *for* your kids, and a legacy is something you leave *in* them." Too often we view legacy solely in terms of material possessions. While wealth can be part of your legacy, it shouldn't be the entirety of your legacy.

Recently I was having coffee with my friend Jeff Galley, and we were discussing the topic of legacy. Jeff shared with me how much he enjoyed attending a recent family gathering to celebrate his grandfather's 90th birthday. As he listened to stories from kids and grandkids about the joy of growing up with Grandpa's influence in their lives, Jeff came to a powerful conclusion: you don't have to live a life of notoriety to live a life that matters. Too often we equate legacy with fame or notoriety. The truth is, for most people, legacy will be filled with shades of anonymity.

But that doesn't diminish its impact. Jeff went on to describe to me the success and the health of so many people in his family, all of which could be traced back to his grandfather's quiet, yet profound, influence.

True legacy has three dimensions to it, revolving around a central value: character *(who you are)*, contribution *(what you've done)*, and connections *(who you've impacted)* with a central focus on eternal value *(why you do it)*. The following pyramid illustrates how the parts of legacy connect to each other:

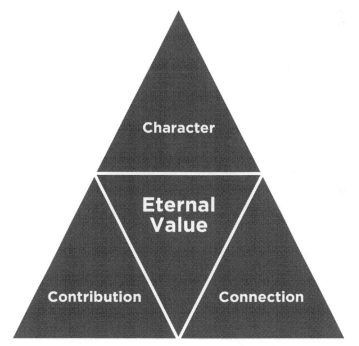

Character (Who you are) — The first dimension of legacy revolves around you as a person. Your character consists of integrity, spirituality, and pliability. It's about how you live, who you follow, and your willingness to cooperate with God's life-shaping process. People will remember you for your character because it provides stability to your legacy.

There's nothing worse than somebody making significant contributions but having a personal life that's a wreck. When it comes to the kind of life you live, character is the proof in the pudding.

Contribution (What you've done) — The second dimension of legacy is the contribution you make to God's Kingdom and to society. Usually this contribution occurs through your time, talent, and treasure. It's the process of leveraging these God-given resources to make a difference in the world. The contribution part of legacy views resources through the lens of biblical stewardship. Rather than spending your time, talent, and treasure solely on yourself, you leverage them for the benefit of others. Again, this doesn't mean you'll be famous or have worldwide notoriety. But it does mean you're faithful.

Connection (Who you've impacted) — The third dimension of legacy is defined by the people you love and serve. Connection includes family, friends, mentees, co-workers, employees, neighbors, and even strangers. It's about believing in others, treating them with respect, and investing in their lives. People live forever, which means the connection you make with them has eternal significance.

Eternal Value (Why you do it) — At the center of the Legacy Pyramid is a value for eternity. It's the motivation behind the three ingredients. It's choosing to live, give, and relate in a way that matters to God and matters beyond the here and now. Doing these things for "the least of these" is eternal value (Matthew 25:31–46). Sharing the hope of Christ with your connections is eternal value. Leveraging your God-given resources for God-glorifying purposes is eternal value. Laying up treasure in heaven is eternal value. Choosing to live a Christ-centered life is eternal value.

Disruptions and Legacy

No matter what disruption you're facing, it's likely to shape your legacy. For some, a crisis casts a dark shadow over their legacy. Unfortunately, one bad mistake (or sin) can permanently define a person's legacy. The thought of "finishing well" may seem impossible.

For others, a disruption serves as a turning point for the things we've discussed in this book. It's a catalyst for prayer, trust, perspective, family, community, or your purpose. Regardless of which side of the legacy coin you find yourself on, you have to answer one question: how will my unexpected disruption shape my character, contribution, and connection from this point forward?

> People may not remember the size of the rocks that unexpectedly rained on your life, but they will remember how you responded to them – good or bad.

Your response to the disruption is a legacy-defining moment. Thinking clearly in this moment is crucial. People may not remember the size of the rocks that unexpectedly rained on your life, but they will remember how you responded to them — good or bad. To help you find clarity of thought, take the "one" test:

- In *one month*, will I feel good about my response, or will I be reeling from the consequences of my response?

- In *one year*, will I be able to positively leverage my response as a teaching moment for others?

- In *one lifetime*, will I be remembered for choosing the right response?

Choosing Your Legacy

I [Karen] had to make this choice after the robbery. Was I going to become a hermit, withdraw from people, and isolate myself in my pain? Was I going to let my response to this devastating incident negatively define my legacy? Or was I going to live? *Truly live?*

My response was slow and difficult. Navigating the emotions afterward was the hardest thing I ever did. But I realized I couldn't allow my past to permanently imprison my legacy. Eventually Stephen and I were married. A couple of years later, Ashley was born. After a few years of working in various jobs, I returned to school to complete my undergraduate degree. Upon graduation, I started teaching in a local public school at an alternative campus for at-risk students. During that season, I discovered that teaching was as much about helping students emotionally as it was about their education.

> **The immense pain I suffered years ago is now a leverage point for me to help others. What was meant for harm in my life, God is now using for good in the lives of others.**

As I reflect on the boys who participated in that robbery, I know now that they must have been at-risk students. I don't think it was an accident that I eventually taught in an at-risk school. And I loved it. In fact, after teaching for a few years, I decided to pursue a Master of Education degree in counseling. Initially, the robbery didn't have anything to do with this choice. But after I got into teaching, I discovered how much I enjoyed working with at-risk students and the emotional side of their lives. I realized how much I enjoyed helping students talk about and navigate their struggles in life.

Today I'm a school counselor, and because of the robbery, as well as my experience with at-risk students, I can now spot at-risk students in the school where I work. I see the path they could choose, and it gives me the opportunity to intervene in their situations long before they can even start getting into serious trouble. The immense pain I suffered years ago is now a leverage point for me to help others. What was meant for harm in my life, God is now using for good in the lives of others. But it started with a choice. And that's where it starts for you, too.

Takeaway #7

The final takeaway when life disrupts your plans is this: **Choose the character, contribution, and connection to finish well.** Creating your legacy is compounded by the choices you make every day. Your choices about character, contribution, and connection are critically important. Making those decisions with eternity in view is even more important. That's what helps you finish well.

Disruptions can be opportunities or obstacles. Our response to them determines the path we will take. What kind of legacy will you write while you still have time? Our challenge to you is to choose the high road. Choose the path with consequences that you will later rejoice over. Make choices that one month, one year, and one lifetime from now will positively impact those around you.

You are in control of you. Nobody else should have control over the legacy you will leave. Choose it wisely and then write it carefully. As you do, a beautiful legacy will unfold in your wake, and the unexpected will transform into the unimaginable. As we close our journey together, may the words of the psalmist pull you one step further out of your pain, and compel you to write an honorable legacy for future generations:

Teach us to realize the brevity of life, so that we may grow in wisdom. O Lord, come back to us! How long will you delay? Take pity on your servants! Satisfy us each morning with your unfailing love, so we may sing for joy to the end of our lives. Give us gladness in proportion to our former misery! Replace the evil years with good. Let us, your servants, see you work again; let our children see your glory. And may the Lord our God show us his approval and make our efforts successful. Yes, make our efforts successful! (Psalm 90:12-17, NLT)

A Prayer of Legacy

Heavenly Father,
Thank you that I still have the opportunity to write my legacy!
Today, I choose to move forward with my life. I won't be held
captive by my past or by my pain. Help me to live with character
and integrity. Empower me to make a contribution that matters
in my world. Use me to invest in relationships and to enrich the lives
of other people. Above all, help me to wisely steward the days
that I have left, and to live each day with eternity in mind.
In Jesus' name I pray, amen.

AFTERWORD

We've done our best to be as transparent as possible about our stories. We've shared the good and the bad, the ups and the downs, and what God has done in our lives in the process. Still, some days are better than others. You never forget major disruptions in your life. You never forget walking through a hailstorm where the sharp rocks of unexpected pain pierce your life. But like anything else, you have to choose the life you're going to live. You have to choose to learn the lessons you can from those disruptions. That's where wisdom comes from.

As you navigate your own disruptions, we hope the seven takeaways we've offered you will help you in your journey. For some of you, the disruptions in your life probably make ours look like a cakewalk. All we can do is share from our own experience and offer you our thoughts from the road we're walking on.

When life disrupts your plans, you will experience some kind of pain. That's inevitable (John 16:33). But again, your response to the unexpected is fully within your control. Do your best to avoid rash decisions. Slow and steady usually leads to better outcomes and fewer regrets. As you pray, God will lead you, help you, and comfort you. When you trust God by acknowledging him and his wisdom, you'll find the peace to face your fears. As you take a few steps back and learn to frame your disruptions with the right perspective, you'll make better decisions. During this journey, lean on your family and on your community of friends. And before you move on with your life, determine how you want your disruption to shape your purpose and your legacy.

Your disruptions didn't necessarily come from God, yet he's the one we're most tempted to blame (1 Corinthians 10:13). It's okay to ask God questions. He's not afraid of your questions, or of the raw emotions you're feeling right now. In fact, he's very interested in hearing from you. Rather than running *from* God, run *to* him. It's in God that you'll find hope, comfort, and the strength to move on. After all, isn't that what you ultimately need?

As you heal, God will even leverage your pain to do good things if you'll let him. That might seem impossible right now. We're simply speaking from our own experiences. God has, and is, doing just that. If you'll cooperate with his life-shaping process, he'll do more in you — and he'll accomplish greater things *through* you.

God is not your enemy. He's the one who can make you whole. May the words of the apostle Paul encourage you:

"Don't fret or worry. Instead of worrying, pray. Let petitions and praises shape your worries into prayers, letting God know your concerns. Before you know it, a sense of God's wholeness, everything coming together for good, will come and settle you down. It's wonderful what happens when Christ displaces worry at the center of your life" (Philippians 4:6–7, MSG).

OVERVIEW OF THE 7 TAKEAWAYS
What to Do When Life Disrupts Your Plans

1. Use prayer as worship and as a weapon when the unexpected appears.

2. Trust God by acknowledging him and acting on his wisdom.

3. Choose to see what others can't see, so you can be what others won't be.

4. Relinquish regret and relate to, or restore, your family.

5. Cultivate community before, during, and after the storm.

6. Discover and pursue God's purpose that will outlast your pain.

7. Choose the character, contribution, and connection to finish well.

ACKNOWLEDGEMENTS

Jesus – Thank you for not abandoning us when life disrupts our plans. Instead, your comforting presence is forming and fulfilling a greater purpose in us and through us.

Ashley – Thank you for your love and support. We couldn't be more proud of you. No matter what life brings your way, always remember that God is faithful and trustworthy. He's preparing you for a wonderful future. We love you!

Parents – Thank you to our parents – Sal & Merle Blandino and Roy & Pearla Thomson – for your extraordinary love, support, prayers, and encouragement during and after the darkest hours of these crises.

Brothers & Sisters – Thank you Chris & Ruth, Mike & Jessie, Eric & Nikki, and Bo & Jessica for your prayers and presence as we navigated these unexpected events.

Friends – So many of our friends have shown extraordinary amounts of love and compassion: prayer, encouraging messages, hugs, hospital visits, hours in waiting rooms, preparing meals, taking time off work. We are overwhelmed with your generosity and kindness. To so many friends, we are forever indebted to you.

7 City Church – Thank you Klen and Audrey Kuruvilla, and everyone at 7 City Church, for praying, serving faithfully, and showing amazing compassion. We love you!

Christ Church – Thank you Pastor Darius and Cindy Johnston, and everyone at Christ Church, who prayed and provided direction and assistance during and after our crises.

Medical Team – Thank you Dr. Parrish for being at Harris Southwest when I needed you most. Your quick diagnosis saved my life. Thank you Dr. Lin, and everybody on the operating team, for your extraordinary surgical wisdom and care. And thank you to all of the nurses and medical staff who served faithfully to help me heal.

Brannon Golden – Thank you for your amazing mentorship. Your editing genius is a gift. Thank you for helping us write better, so that we could share our stories with others.

NOTES

1 Mark Batterson, *The Circle Maker*, (Grand Rapids, MI: Zondervan, 2011), 53.

2 Mark Batterson, *In a Pit with a Lion on a Snowy Day*, (Colorado Springs, CO: Multnomah Books, 2006), 98.

3 Rick Warren, *The Purpose Driven Life*, (Grand Rapids, MI: Zondervan, 2002), 118.

4 Randy Frazee, *The Connecting Church*, (Grand Rapids, MI: Zondervan, 2001), 45.

5 Rick Warren, *The Purpose Driven Life*, (Grand Rapids, MI: Zondervan, 2002), 132.

6 Rob Ketterling, *Change Before You Have To*, (Springfield, MO: Influence Resources, 2012), 87.

7 Charles Colson and Nancy Pearcey, *How Now Shall We Live?*, (Carol Stream, IL: Tyndale House Publishers, Inc., 1999), 33.

8 Os Hillman, *The 9 to 5 Window: How Faith Can Transform the Workplace*, (Ventura, CA: Regal Books, 2005), 23.

9 Gene Edward Veith, Jr., *God at Work: Your Christian Vocation in All of Life*, (Wheaton, IL: Crossway, 2002), 19.

ABOUT THE AUTHORS

STEPHEN BLANDINO is the lead pastor of 7 City Church, an author, blogger, and coach. With over 20 years of experience in local church and nonprofit leadership, Stephen is passionate about helping people engage in personal growth, develop their full leadership capacity, and produce effective, Kingdom-advancing ministry. He holds a Master's in Organizational Leadership. Stephen lives in the Fort Worth, Texas, area with his wife, Karen, and their daughter, Ashley.

KAREN BLANDINO is a counselor in the public school system. She holds a Master's of Education in Counseling from TCU, and an undergraduate degree from UTA. Karen enjoys travelling and spending time with her family and friends.

Contact Stephen & Karen Blandino

Stephen Blandino blogs regularly at **stephenblandino.com** and is available to speak on personal growth and leadership topics for keynote, half-day, and full day events. He also provides coaching opportunities and consulting. To learn more, or to contact Stephen or Karen, connect with them at:

Blog: stephenblandino.com

Twitter: twitter.com/stephenblandino

Twitter: twitter.com/kblandino

Facebook: facebook.com/stephen.blandino

Facebook: facebook.com/karen.t.blandino

UNEXPECTED:
What to Do When Life Disrupts Your Plans

Study Guide

By Stephen & Karen Blandino

(5 Sessions)

Everybody encounters the "unexpected" – losing a job, receiving a bad report from a doctor, a tragic accident, a late-night phone call, a relationship ending, a financial setback, or even the death of a loved one. The question is, how do we respond when life unexpectedly disrupts our plans?

In this five-session study guide (for small groups or personal study), Stephen and Karen Blandino share their personal stories of the unexpected. Karen shares how her peace was stolen during a robbery when five young men broke into her house, and then dragged her out of the shower at gunpoint. Stephen shares his journey of simultaneous congestive heart failure and pulmonary failure despite years of annual check-ups with good reports.

From their stories, Stephen and Karen share valuable lessons on trust, perspective, community, purpose, and legacy that you can apply to your life today. Whether you're navigating an unexpected disruption, or your life is going great, these practical lessons will foster hope, strength, wisdom, and a closer relationship with Christ.

Available from Amazon.com, BarnesandNoble.com, Booksamillion.com, and StephenBlandino.com

GO! Starting a Personal Growth Revolution
By Stephen Blandino

Five Steps to Unlock Your Growth and Inspire Growth in Others

Do you want to close the gap between who you are and who you want to be? Do you want to help your friends, co-workers, or employees grow to their full potential. In *GO! Starting a Personal Growth Revolution*, Stephen Blandino guides you through the five levels of personal growth, and equips you with the practices to maximize growth within you and around you. No matter how you want to grow, *GO!* provides the inspiration and the roadmap to help you take your next step.

"Some books are written to inform, and others to inspire, still others to motivate you to action. In GO! Starting a Personal Growth Revolution *author Stephen Blandino does all three. You will learn, grow and move forward. The concepts are real-life and the strategies, if followed, will actualize your full capacity potential."*

DR. SAMUEL R. CHAND
Leadership Coach, Consultant, and Author of *Cracking Your Church's Culture Code*
(www.samchand.com)

"Anybody who wants to become all that God wants them to be has to read GO! *Stephen hits the nail on the head on how we develop personally so that we can maximize our God given potential!"*

HERBERT COOPER
Lead Pastor, People's Church, Oklahoma City

"In business I'm always looking for a competitive edge, and in GO! Starting a Personal Growth Revolution *Stephen Blandino gives you that edge. Through the five levels of personal growth you create a pathway for personal growth both for yourself and the people you lead. This book is one you'll actually implement the wisdom it contains."*

BILL BARNETT
Nationally Syndicated Radio Host and the Best Selling Author of
Are You DUMB Enough to be RICH?

**Available from Amazon.com, BarnesandNoble.com,
Booksamillion.com, and StephenBlandino.com**

Creating Your Church's Culture:
How to Uproot Mediocrity and Create a Healthy Organizational Culture

By Stephen Blandino

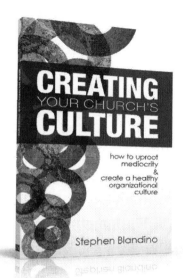

How do you create a thriving organizational culture in your church? Churches are committed to a spiritual mission, but it is often the organizational aspects of the church that hinder the mission from moving forward. In *Creating Your Church's Culture,* you'll learn how to define your culture, activate the culture equation, infuse your values into your culture, create a learning culture, develop effective systems, increase employee and volunteer engagement, measure the health of your culture, and uproot bureaucracy. This practical book is loaded with wisdom and inspiration to help you improve the organizational aspects of your church's culture. Plus, the book includes a culture assessment and implementation guide to help you apply what you're learning.

"Concise, strategic, and practical! Stephen Blandino gives you the roadmap you need to develop a healthy organizational culture with fully engaged team members."

Scott Wilson, Pastor of The Oaks Fellowship and author of *Ready, Set, Grow: 3 Conversations that Will Bring Lasting Growth to Your Church*

"Too often we make leading a church more complicated than it ought to be. *Creating Your Church's Culture* is an honest look at how to accomplish the mission of the church with more simplicity. Readable, practical, and insightful."

Jeff Galley, Team Leader for Life Groups and Missions, LifeChurch.tv

Available from Amazon.com, BarnesandNoble.com, Booksamillion.com, and StephenBlandino.com